PONY TRACKS

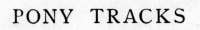

THE LAST STAND

PONY TRACKS

WRITTEN AND
ILLUSTRATED BY

FREDERIC REMINGTON

American Legacy Press • *New York*

This 1982 edition is published by American Legacy Press,
distributed by Crown Publishers, Inc.

Manufactured in the United States of America

Library of Congress Cataloging in Publication Data

Remington, Frederic, 1861-1909.
  Pony tracks.
  Reprint. Originally published: New York : Harper,
1895.
  1. West (U.S.)—Description and travel—1880-1950.
2. Frontier and pioneer life—West (U.S.) 3. Indians of
North America—Wars—1866-1895. 4. Chihuahua (Mexico :
State)—Description and travel. 5. Remington, Frederic,
1861-1909. I. Title.
F595.R38   1982   978   82-6834
                               AACR2

ISBN: 0-517-386283
h g f e d c b a

CONTENTS

ILLUSTRATIONS

FOREWORD

A restless, adventurous breed of men was responsible for enriching American culture and vivifying American history—a breed of men who dedicated their lives to a creative and historical mission.

Frederic Sackrider Remington, born in Canton, New York, in 1861, was of that breed. He turned his dreams into reality by shedding light on the dark pages of the American West through his drawings, sculpture and writing.

Adventure was in the Remington blood. His father, Seth Pierre Remington, was a newspaper publisher who left his profession to establish a distinguished military record in the Civil War and then later resumed his career in publishing. Coming from that same Remington mold, young Frederic learned to ride horses, developed fine athletic skills and a talent for art and was inbred with a roaming spirit which caused Remington's educational history to be one of inconsistency. There was another vision, another purpose in life, that directed his energies elsewhere. He was sent to Yale to study art but excelled in football and boxing. In 1880 his father died and he quit school.

Around this time he fell in love with Eva Adele Caten, but her father refused to grant her hand in marriage because of Remington's unsuccessful station in life as an artist. Propelled by his fascination of the West and the rejection of marriage, Remington, with his father's inheritance money, headed out to Montana to seek his fortune in gold. Prospecting, however, was unsuccessful, as Remington was distracted by a consuming interest in the way of life he found there. The brawn and vitality of the West made an overwhelming impression on him. For five

years Remington was a vagabond on the western trails, drawing, writing, and living out chapters of American history. Remington was very generous and foolhardy with his inheritance
and was not making a living from his drawings and paintings.
In 1884 he finally married Eva Caten and they moved near Kansas City, Kansas. Times got tougher as Remington struggled
through a bad investment deal and a substantial lack of income.
He sent his wife back East and once again took up the search for
gold, this time in the Southwest. As before, he drifted from his
search to continue his artistic mission.

Finally, when all his money ran out, Remington decided to
pack up his paintings, drawings and souvenirs and move to New
York City. Within a few months, an illustration of his was on
the cover of *Harper's Weekly* with full credit. From then on, he
became a regular staff artist and writer. Success was knocking at
his door. He went on to become one of the most popular and
best-paid artists of his time, a critically acclaimed sculptor and
a successful writer.

Remington wrote a fairly popular novel called *John Ermine of
the Yellowstone* and had seven books published that were com-
piled from his numerous magazine pieces. The first one of these
compilations was published in 1895 under the title *Pony Tracks*.
Fifteen of his best narratives are represented here in an exciting,
realistic, journalistic style as opposed to the glorified and
romanticized style of other writers. And he drew most of his
illustrations to accompany his words.

In *Pony Tracks*, one can relive Remington's adventures in the
West. One of the author's favorite pieces included in the collection, "Black Water and Shallows," takes one through the north
country with a fresh view of the untapped wilderness and a daring sense of adventure. He covers the Indian Wars period with
such startling pieces as "The Sioux Outbreak in South Dakota"
and "Lieutenant Casey's Last Scout." As the Indian Wars died
down and the West was becoming civilized, Remington, in
order to keep his stories fresh and exciting, had to stay on the
move. The army had been reduced to a peace-keeping unit and
the cowboys had to move to new frontiers. Remington followed
their trail through the Southwest and Mexico and came up with

such accounts as "In the Sierra Madre with the Punchers," "A Rodeo at Los Ojos" and "Coaching in Chihuahua."

Remington excluded no one in his writings. They were all there—the generals, the cowboys, the Indians, the good, the bad, the renowned and the common man. American history owes much to people like Frederic Remington, for it is they who have made our history a unique collective experience. Remington dedicated *Pony Tracks* "to the fellows who rode the ponies that made the tracks." It was a dedication that could equally have been directed to the author, who was there to ride alongside them and immortalize them for posterity.

New York   GEORGE GESNER
1982

PONY TRACKS

CHASING A MAJOR-GENERAL

THE car had been side-tracked at Fort Keough, and on the following morning the porter shook me, and announced that it was five o'clock. An hour later I stepped out on the rear platform, and observed that the sun would rise shortly, but that meanwhile the air was chill, and that the bald, square-topped hills of the "bad lands" cut rather hard against the gray of the morning. Presently a trooper galloped up with three led horses, which he tied to a stake. I inspected them, and saw that one had a "cow saddle," which I recognized as an experiment suggested by the general. The animal bearing it had a threatening look, and I expected a repetition of a performance of a few days before, when I had chased the general for over three hours, making in all twenty-eight miles.

Before accepting an invitation to accompany an Indian commission into the Northwest I had asked the general quietly if this was a "horseback" or a "wagon outfit." He had assured me that he was not a "wagon man," and I indeed had heard before that he was not. There is always a distinction in the army between wagon men and men who go without wagons by transporting their supplies on pack animals. The wagon men have always acquired more reputation as travellers than Indian fighters. In a trip to the Pine Ridge Agency I had discovered that General Miles was not committed to any strained theory

of how mounted men should be moved. Any settled purpose he might have about his movements were all locked
up in a desperate desire to "get thar." Being a little late
in leaving a point on the railroad, I rode along with Lieutenant Guilfoil, of the Ninth, and we moved at a gentle
trot. Presently we met a citizen in a wagon, and he,
upon observing the lieutenant in uniform, pulled up his
team and excitedly inquired,

"What's the matter, Mr. Soldier?"

Guilfoil said nothing was the matter that he knew of.

"Who be you uns after?"

"No one," replied the lieutenant.

"Well, I just saw a man go whirling up this 'ere valley
with a soldier tearin' after him fit to kill" (that was the
general's orderly), "and then comes a lot more soldiers
just a-smokin', and I sort of wondered what the man had
done."

We laughed, and remarked that the general must be
riding pretty hard. Other citizens we met inquired if
that man was a lunatic or a criminal. The idea of the
soldiers pursuing a man in citizen's clothes furthered the
idea, but we assured them that it was only General Miles
going somewhere.

All of these episodes opened my eyes to the fact that
if I followed General Miles I would have to do some
riding such as I had rarely done before. In coming back
to the railroad we left the Pine Ridge Agency in the
evening without supper, and I was careful to get an even
start. My horse teetered and wanted to gallop, but I
knew that the twenty-eight miles would have to be done
at full speed, so I tried to get him down to a fast trot,
which gait I knew would last better; but in the process
of calming him down to a trot I lost sight of the general and his orderly as they went tearing like mad over

GENERAL MILES AND HIS ESCORT

THE SUPPLY TRAIN

a hill against the last gleam of the sunset. I rode at a very rapid trot over the hills in the moonlight for over three hours, but I never saw the general again until I met him at dinner. Then I further concluded that if I followed the general I would have no time to regait my horses, but must take them as I found them, gallop or trot. So on this cool morning at Keough I took observations of the horses which were tied to the post, with my mind full of misgivings.

Patter, patter, patter—clank, clank, clank; up comes the company of Cheyenne scouts who are to escort the general—fine-looking, tall young men, with long hair, and mounted on small Indian ponies. They were dressed and accoutred as United States soldiers, and they fill the eye of a military man until nothing is lacking. Now the general steps out of the car and hands the commission into a six-mule ambulance. I am given a horse, and, mounting, we move off over the plain and into the hills. The sun comes streaming over the landscape, and the general is thinking about this old trail, and how years before he had ploughed his way through the blinding snow to the Lame Deer fight. I am secretly wishing that it would occupy his mind more fully, so that my breakfast might settle at the gentle gait we are going, but shortly he says, " It's sixty miles, and we must move along." We break into a gallop. The landscape is gilded by the morning sun, and the cool of the October air makes it a perfect thing, but there are elements in the affair which complicate its perfection. The " bad lands " are rough, and the general goes down a hill with even more rapidity than up it. The horses are not the perfect animals of the bridle-path, but poor old cavalry brutes, procured by the government under the old contract system, by which the government pays something like $125 for a $60 horse. This could be remedied by allowing the officers of each regiment to buy their own horses; but in our army nothing is remedied, because a lot of nice old gentlemen in Washington are too conservative to do anything but eat and sleep. There is a bit of human nature at the bottom of our army organization, and where is the man who can change that? Men who were the very jewels of the profession years ago have reached in due time the upper grades of rank, and occupy the bureaus of the department. These men who have acquired rank, years, and discretion naturally do nothing, and with sedate gravity insist that no one else shall do anything. The ambitious young men have to wait patiently for their retirement, and in process of waiting they, too, become old and conservative. Old soldiers are pardonable rubbish, since soldiers, like other men, must age and decay, the only distinction being that youthful vigor is of prime importance to a soldier, while in the case of the citizen any abatement of vigor is rewarded by being shelved. What to do with old soldiers is a problem which I will hand over to the economists as being beyond my depth. But to return to the going downhill. General Miles has acquired his knowledge of riding from wild Indians, and wild Indians go uphill and downhill as a matter of course at whatever gait they happen to be travelling. He would make his horse climb a tree with equal gravity if he was bound that way. The general has known Indians to ride for two days and a night at a rapid gallop, and it never occurs to him that he cannot do anything which any one else can; so he spurs along, and we go cutting around the *coulies* and bluffs like frightened antelopes or mad creatures. The escort strings out behind. This is observed with a grim humor by the general, who desires nothing so much as to leave his escort far in the rear. He turns in his saddle, and seeing the dust of the escort far behind, says: "Shake up the young men a little; do 'em good. They get sleepy;" and away we go.

It is over thirty miles to the first relay station, or courier's camp, and another problem looms up. The general's weight is over two hundred pounds, and I confess to two hundred and fifteen avoirdupois, and, as I have before remarked, my horse was not an Irish hunter, so my musing took a serious vein. It is all very well for a major-general to ride down a cavalry horse, but if such an accident were to happen to me, then my friends in the cavalry would crown me with thorns. Two hundred and fifteen pounds requires a great deal more careful attention than a one-hundred-and-forty-pound wasp-waisted cavalryman. What the latter can do with impunity would put me on foot—a thing that happened some ten years since in this very State of Montana, and a thing I have treasured in mind, and will not have repeated. So I brought the old horse down to a trot, and a good round trot eats up a road in short order. Your galloper draws away from you, but if the road is long enough, you find that you are at his heels.

After a good day's ride of something like sixty miles, we met a troop of the Eighth Cavalry near its camp on the Tongue River, and the general is escorted in. The escorts draw into line, salute, and the general is duly deposited in a big Sibley tent; and I go away on the arms of some "cavalry kids" (as young lieutenants are called) to a hole in the ground (a dugout) where they are quartered. On the following morning I am duly admonished that if my whereabouts could have been ascertained on the previous evening, the expedition would have continued to the camp of the First Cavalry. I do not think the general was unduly severe, desiring simply to shift

the responsibility of the procrastination on to other
shoulders, and meanwhile being content to have things as
they were. I was privately thanked by the citizen members of the commission for the delay I had caused, since
they had a well - grounded conviction that sixty miles a
day in an army ambulance was trouble enough. After
some sarcasm by a jolly young sub, to the effect that " if
one wants to call a citizen out of a tent, one must ring a
dinner-bell," we were again mounted and on the way. I
was badly mounted that day, but able to participate in
the wild charge of forty - five miles to the Lame Deer
camp, near the Cheyenne Agency. The fifty Cheyenne
scouts and a troop of the Eighth were in escort.

By a happy combination I was able to add greatly to
my equestrian knowledge on this ride. It happened in
this way; but I must explain. Some years ago I had
occasion to ride a stock saddle (the cowboy article), and
with all the positiveness of immature years, I held all
other trees and all other methods of riding in a magnificent contempt. Later on I had to be convinced that a
great many young cavalry officers in our service were the
most daring and perfect riders, and that the McClelland
saddle was the proper thing. I even elaborated a theory
in explanation of all this, which I had duly shattered for
me when I came East and frequented a New York riding-
academy, where a smiling professor of the art assured me
that cowboys and soldiers were the worst possible riders.
Indeed, the sneers of the polite European were so super-
lative that I dared not even doubt his statements. Of
course I never quite understood how my old champions
of the cattle range and the war trail could pick things off
the ground while in full career, or ride like mad over the
cut banks and bowlders, if they were such desperately bad
riders ; and I never was able to completely understand

why my European master could hardly turn in his saddle without tumbling off. But still he reduced me to submission, and I ceased even to doubt. I changed my style of riding, in deference to a public sentiment, and got my legs tucked up under my chin, and learned to loose my seat at every alternate footfall, and in time acquired a balance which was as secure as a pumpkin on the side of a barrel. Thus equipped with all this knowledge and my own saddle, I went out to the Northwest with the purpose of introducing a little revolution in cavalry riding. Things went swimmingly for a time. The interpreters and scouts watched my riding with mingled pity and scorn, but I knew they were unenlightened, and in no way to be regarded seriously. The general was duly amused by my teetering, and suggested to the smiling escort officers that "he has lived so long abroad, you know," etc., all of which I did not mind, for my faith in the eternal art of the thing was complete. Now to tell how I discovered that I was riding a seat which was no seat at all, and was only retained by a series of happy accidents, I will continue. While at the head of the column, where I could see the deep ruts in the road and the bowlders, and could dodge the prairie-dog holes, it was simple enough ; but my horse being a very clumsy galloper, and beginning to blow under the pace, I began to pull up, calculating to get a sharp trot, and overhaul the column when it slowed down. The column of soldiers dashed by, and the great cloud of dust rose up behind them which always follows a herd of animals in the West. Being no longer able to see, the only thing to do under the circumstances was to give my horse his head, and resign myself to the chances of a gopher hole, if it was foreordained that my horse should find one. True to his instincts, my old cavalry horse plunged into the ranks. You cannot keep a troop horse

out of the ranks. They know their place, and seek it
with the exactitude of water. If the cavalry tactics are
ever changed, the present race of horses will have to be
sold, because, while you can teach a horse anything, you
cannot unteach him.

In front I could see two silhouettes of soldiers tearing
along, and behind could hear the heavy pounding of the
troop horses, the clank of arms, the snorts and heavy
breathings. I could hardly see my horse's head, to say
nothing of the ground in front. Here is where the perfect grip with the thighs is wanted, and here is where the
man who is bundled up like a ball on his horse's back is
in imminent danger of breaking his neck. I felt like a
pack on a government mule, and only wished I had some
one to "throw the diamond hitch over me." The inequalities of the road make your horse plunge and go stag-
gering sidewise, or down on his knees, and it is not at all
an unusual thing for a cavalryman to upset entirely,
though nothing short of a total turn-over will separate a
veteran soldier from his horse. After a few miles of
these vicissitudes I gained the head of the column, and
when the pace slackened I turned the whole thing over in
my mind, and a great light seemed to shine through the
whole subject. For a smooth road and a trotting horse,
that European riding-master was right; but when you put
a man in the dust or smoke, over the rocks and cut banks,
on the "bucking" horse, or where he must handle his
weapons or his *vieta*, he must have a seat on his mount as
tight as a stamp on an envelope, and not go washing
around like a shot in a bottle. In a park or on a country
road, where a man has nothing to do but give his undi-
vided attention to sticking on his saddle, it has its advan-
tages. An Indian or a cowboy could take the average
park rider off from his horse, scalp him, hang him on a

UNITED STATES CAVALRY IN WINTER RIG

UNITED STATES INFANTRY IN WINTER RIG

bush, and never break a gallop. I do not wish to seem intolerant, because I will say that the most beautiful horse and the most perfect horseman I have ever seen was the bay gelding Partisan and his rider in the high-school class at the recent Horse Show in New York; but I do insist that no one shall for a moment imagine that the American style of riding is not the firmest of all seats.

With a repetition of the military forms, we reached the cavalry camp on the Lame Deer Creek. This is an old battle-ground of the general's—his last fight with the Cheyennes, where, as the general puts it, we "kicked them out of their blankets in the early morning." These Indians recognize him as their conqueror, and were allied with him in the Nez Percé campaign. One old chief pointed to the stars on his shoulder-strap, and charged him to remember that they helped to put them there.

That night was very cold, and I slept badly, so at an early hour I rolled out of my blankets and crawled into my clothes. I stepped out of my tent, and saw that the stars were yet visible and the light of the morning warming up to chase the gray shadows over the western hills. Three tight little cavalry soldiers came out on the parade, and blew three bugles as hard as ever they could to an unappreciative audience of sleepy soldiers and solemn hills. I walked down past the officers' row, and shook the kinks out of my stiffened knees. Everything was as quietly dismal as only a sleeping camp can be. The Sibley containing General Miles showed no signs of life, and until he arose this little military solar system would not revolve. I bethought me of the irregulars. They were down in the river bottom—Lieutenant Casey and his Indian scouts. I knew that Casey had commanded Indian scouts until his temper was as refined as beaten gold, so I thought it safer to arouse him than any one else, and,

walking down, I scratched at his tent — which is equiva-
lent to knocking — and received a rather loud and surly
inquiry as to what I wanted.   My sensitive nature was so
shocked by this that, like the bad actor, I had hopes for
no more generous gift than a cigarette.   I was let into the
Sibley, and saw the ground covered with blanketed forms.
One of the swathed forms sat up, and the captain allowed
he wanted to get up in the night, but that ever since Lieutenant Blank had shot at the orderly he was afraid to
move about in the gloom.   Lieutenant B. sat up and de-
nied the impeachment.   Another officer arose and made
some extended remarks on the unseemly disturbance at
this unseasonable hour.   To pass over these inequalities
of life, I will say that the military process of stiffening a
man's backbone and reducing his mind to a logarithm
breeds a homogeneous class whom we all know.   They
have small waists, and their clothes fit them; they are
punctilious; they respect forms, and always do the digni-
fied and proper thing at the particular instant, and never
display their individuality except on two occasions : one
is the field of battle and the other is before breakfast.
Some bright fellow will one day tell in print the droll stock
anecdotes of the United States army, and you'll all agree
that they are good.   They are better, though, if you sit
in a Sibley on a cold morning while the orderly boils
the coffee ; and are more fortunate if you have Ned Casey
to embellish what he calls the international complications
which arose from the bombardment of Canada with pav-
ing-stones by a drunken recruit at Detroit.

After the commission had talked to a ring of drowsy
old chiefs, and the general had reminded them that he
had thrashed them once, and was perfectly willing to do
it again if they did not keep in the middle of the big
road, the commission was loaded into the ambulances.

The driver clucked and whistled and snapped his whip as a preliminary which always precedes the concerted movement of six mules, and we started. This time I found that I had a mount that was "a horse from the ground up," as they phrase it in the red-blooded West. Well it was so, for at the relay camp I had issued to me a sorrel ruin which in the pristine vigor of its fifth year would not have commanded the value of a tin cup. After doing a mile of song and dance on this poor beast I dismounted, and shifting my saddle back to my led horse of the morning, which was led by a Crow scout, made the sixty-mile march of that day on the noble animal. Poor old chap, fit for a king, good for all day and the next, would bring six hundred dollars in the New York Horse Exchange, but condemned to pack a trooper in the ranks until a penurious government condemns and sells him to a man who, nine times out of ten, by the law of God, ought not to be intrusted with the keeping of the meanest of his creatures, to say nothing of his noblest work— a horse. "Such is life," is the salve a good soldier puts on his wounds.

During the day we went all over the battle-field of the Little Big Horn. I heard a good deal of professional criticism, and it is my settled conviction that had Reno and Benteen gone in and fought as hard as they were commanded to do, Custer would have won his fight, and to-day be a major-general. The military moral of that affair for young soldiers is that when in doubt about what to do it is always safe to go in and fight "till you drop," remembering that, however a citizen may regard the proposition, a soldier cannot afford to be anything else than a "dead lion."

We were nearing the Crow Agency and Fort Custer, and it is against all my better impulses, and with trepidation at the impropriety of unveiling the truth, that I disclose the fact that the general would halt the column at a convenient distance from a post, and would then exchange his travel-worn garb for glittering niceties of a major-general's uniform. The command then advanced into the fort. The guns bellowed and the cavalry swung into line, while numerous officers gathered, in all the perfection of neat-fitting uniforms, to receive him. At this time the writer eliminated himself from the ceremonial, and from some point of vantage proceeded to pull up his boots so as to cover as much as possible the gaping wounds in his riding-trousers, and tried vainly to make a shooting-jacket fit like an officer's blouse, while he dealt his hat sundry thumps in a vain endeavor to give it a more rakish appearance. He was then introduced and apologized for in turn. To this day he hopes the mantle of charity was broad enough to cover his case.

What a contrast between soldiers in field and soldiers in garrison! Natty and trim — as straight as a sapling, with few words and no gestures—quite unlike those of two days, or rather nights, ago, when the cold froze them out of their blankets, and they sat around the camp-fires pounding tin cans and singing the Indian medicine song with a good Irish accent. Very funny that affair—the mixture of Cheyenne and Donnybrook is a strange noise.

The last stage from Custer to the railroad is thirty-five miles and a half, which we did with two relays, the latter half of it in the night. There was no escort— only two orderlies and the general—and I pattered along through the gloom. The clouds hung over the earth in a dense blanket, and the road was as dim as a Florentine fresco; but night nor cold nor heat can bring General Miles to a walk, and the wild charge in the dark was, as an experience, a complete thing. You cannot see; you whirl through a cañon cut in the mud; you plough through the sage-brush and over the rocks clatter and bang. The general is certainly a grim old fellow—one of the kind that make sparks fly when he strikes an obstacle. I could well believe the old Fifth Infantryman who said "he's put many a corn on a dough-boy's foot," and it's a red-letter day for any one else that keeps at his horse's heels. You may ride into a hole, over a precipice, to perdition, if it's your luck on this night, but is not the general in front? You follow the general—that's the grand idea—that is the military idea. If the United States army was strung out in line with its general ahead, and if he should ride out into the broad Atlantic and swim to sea, the whole United States army would follow along, for that's the idea, you know.

But for the headlong plunge of an orderly, we passed through all right, with due thankfulness on my part, and got to our car at the siding, much to the gratification of the Chicago colored man in charge, who found life at Custer Station a horrid blank. Two hundred and forty-eight miles in thirty-six hours and a half, and sixty miles of it on one horse, was not bad riding, considering everything. Not enough to make a man famous or lame, but enough for the time being.

LIEUTENANT CASEY'S LAST SCOUT

ON THE HOSTILE FLANKS WITH THE CHIS-CHIS-CHASH

THE train bearing the Cheyenne scout corps pulled into Rapid City somewhat late. It is possible you may think that it was a train of Pullman palace cars, but you would be mistaken, for it was a freight train, with the horses in tight box-cars, the bacon and Chis-chis-chash * on flat gravel cars, and Lieutenants Casey and Getty in the caboose. Evidently the element of haste was woven into this movement. We were glad to meet again. Expansive smiles lit up the brown features of the Indian scouts as they recognized me. Old Wolf-Voice came around in his large, patronizing way and said, " How?— what you do out here?" Wolf-Voice was a magnificent type of the Indian, with a grand face, a tremendous physique, and enough self-containment for a High-Church bishop. High-Walking nudged Stump-Horn and whispered in his ear, and they both smiled as they looked at me. Lieutenant Casey walked out in the road and talked with General Miles, who sat on his beautiful sorrel horse, while two scouts and a young " horse-pusher " † from St. Louis helped me to load one strawberry-roan horse, branded " 52 " on the nigh front foot, into a box-car with a

* The name the Cheyennes apply to themselves.
† Boy who travels with horses on the cars.

scrawny lot of little ponies, who showed the hard scouting of the last month in their lank quarters.

The quartermaster came down and asked Lieutenant Casey for a memorandum of his outfit, which was " 70 horses, 49 Indian scouts, 1 interpreter, 2 white officers, 1000 pounds of bacon, so many crackers, 2000 pounds forage, 5 Sibley tents, and 1 citizen," all of which the quartermaster put down in a little book. You are not allowed by United States quartermasters to have an exaggerated estimate of your own importance. Bacon and forage and citizens all go down in the same column, with the only distinction that the bacon and forage outnumber you.

We were pulled down the road a few miles to the town of Hermoso, and there, in the moonlight, the baggage was unloaded and the wild little ponies frightened out of the cars, down a chute, into the stock corrals. The Sibleys were pitched, and a crowd of curious citizens, who came down to feast their eyes on the Chis-chis-chash, were dissipated when a rather frugal dinner was prepared. This was Christmas night, and rather a cheerless one, since, in the haste of departure, the Sibley stoves had been forgotten. We never had stoves again until the gallant Leavenworth battalion came to the rescue with their surplus, and in the cold, frosty nights in the foot-hills there can be no personal happiness where there are no stoves. We brewed a little mess of hot stuff in a soldier's tin cup, and, in the words of Private Mulvaney, we drank to the occasion, "three fingers — standing up !"

The good that comes in the ill wind where stoves are lacking is that you can get men up in the morning. Sun-worship must have originated in circumstances of this kind. The feeling of thankfulness at the sight of the golden rays permeates your soul, and your very bones are made glad.

A few ounces of bacon, some of those accursed crackers which are made to withstand fire, water, and weevil, a quart of coffee blacker than evil, then down come the Sibleys, the blankets are rolled and the saddles adjusted, and bidding *adios* to the First Infantry (which came in during the night), we trot off down the road.

These, then, are the Cheyenne scouts. Well, I am glad I know the fact, but I never can reconcile the trim-looking scout corps of Keogh with these strange-looking objects. Erstwhile their ponies were fat, and cavorted around when falling in ranks; now they paddle along in the humblest kind of a business-like jog-trot. The new overcoats of the corps metamorphose the scouts into something between Russian Cossacks and Black Crooks. Saddle pockets bulge out, and a thousand and one little alterations in accoutrement grow up in the field which are frowned down in garrison. The men have scouted hard for a month, and have lost two nights' sleep, so at the halts for the wagons they lop down in the dust of the road, and sleep, while the little ponies stand over them, ears down, heads hanging, eyes shut, and one hind foot drawn up on its toe. Nothing can look so dejected as a pony, and doubtless few things have more reason to feel so. A short march of twenty-five miles passes us through the Seventeenth Infantry camp under Colonel Offley, and down to the Cheyenne River, where we camp for the night. There is another corps of Cheyenne scouts somewhere here on the river, under Lieutenant L. H. Struthers, of the First Infantry, and we expect to join them. On the other side of the Cheyenne rise the tangled masses of the famous Bad Lands— seamed and serrated, gray here, the golden sunset flash-

CHIS-CHIS-CHASH SCOUT ON THE FLANKS

"TWO GHOSTS I SAW"

ing there, with dark recesses giving back a frightful gloom—a place for stratagem and murder, with nothing to witness its mysteries but the cold blue winter sky. Yet we are going there. It is full of savage Sioux. The sun goes down. I am glad to cease thinking about it.

It is such a mere detail that I will not waste time on it, but this freezing out of your blankets four or five times every night, and this having to go out and coax a cooking fire into a cheerful spirit, can occupy a man's mind so that any words not depraved do not seem of any consequence. During one of the early hours I happened to sleep, and in this interval Mr. Struthers came into our tepee. He had been on a night's ride to the colonel for orders, and in passing, dropped in for a chat with Casey. When about to go, he said,

"Oh, by-the-way, I met Remington."

"Do you want to renew the acquaintance?" replied Casey.

"Why—how—why—yes."

"Well, he's there, on the other side of this tent." And Mr. Struthers passed out in the gloom, and his muttered expressions of astonishment were presently lost in the distance. I had ridden and camped with Mr. Struthers a few days since in the up country, while on the way to "the galloping Sixth."

The next day we passed down the river, and soon saw what to inexperienced eyes might be dark gray rocks on the top of yellow hills. They were the pickets of the Cheyennes, and presently we saw the tepees and the ponies, and then we rode into camp. The men from Tongue River greeted the men from Pine Ridge — the relatives and friends—with *ki-yis* of delight. The corps from Pine Ridge was organized from the Cheyennes on that reservation, and was as yet only partially disciplined, and in no way to be compared with Casey's Old Guard from Tongue River. Some two nights before, the Sioux had fired into their camp, and they had skirmished with the enemy. The vermilion of the war-path was on every countenance, and, through sympathy, I saw that our men too had gone into this style of decorative art; for faces which had previously been fresh and clean now passed my vision streaked and daubed into preternatural ferocity.

It grew late and later, and yet Lieutenant Struthers did not return from his scouting of the day. We were alarmed, and wondered and hoped; for scouting through the Bad Lands to the stronghold was dangerous, to state it mildly. A few shots would not be heard twelve miles away in the hills. We pictured black objects lying prone on the sand as we scouted next day—little masses of clay which had been men and horses, but would then be as silent as the bare hillocks about them.

" Ki-yi-yip—a-ou !" and a patter in the gloom.

" That's Struthers." We fall over each other as we pile out of the hole in the Sibley, and find Struthers and Lieutenant Byrom, of the Eighth Cavalry, all safe and sound.

" We have been on the stronghold; they are all gone; rustle some coffee," are words in the darkness; and we crawl back into the tent, where presently the big, honest, jolly eyes of Mr. Struthers look over a quart cup, and we are happy. Byrom was a fine little cavalryman, and I have good reason to know that for impudent daring of that desperately quiet kind he is distinguished in places where all men are brave.

Away goes the courier to the colonel for orders, and after a time back he comes—a wild dash of twelve miles in the dark, and of little moment here, but a life memory to an unaccustomed one.

"We go on the stronghold in the morning," says Casey; "and now to bed." A bed consists of two blankets spread on the ground, and all the personal property not otherwise appropriated piled on top. A luxury, mind you, is this; later it was much more simple, consisting of earth for a mattress and the sky for a counterpane.

The sun is not up when in comes the horse herd. My strawberry roan goes sneaking about in the frosty willows, and after sundry well-studied manœuvres I get a grip on the lariat, and am lugged and jerked over the brush until "52 on the nigh front foot" consents to stand still. I saddle up, but have lost my gun. I entreat Mr. Thompson, the interpreter, to help me find it. Mr. Thompson is a man who began fighting for the Union in East Tennessee about thirty years long gone, and he has continued to engage in that work up to date. Mr. Thompson has formed a character which is not as round as a ball, but much more the shape of horn-silver in its native state. He is humorous by turns, and early in my acquaintance he undertook the cultivation of my mind in the art of war as practised on the frontier. On this occasion he at last found my Springfield, and handed it to me with the admonition "that in times like these one warrior can't look after another warrior's gun."

The wagons were to go—well, I never knew where, but they went off over the hills, and I never saw them again for some miserable days and dreary nights. Five Pine Ridge Cheyennes and Mr. Wolf-Voice were my party, and we filed away. At Battle Creek we watered, and crossed the Cheyenne a mile above. My horse was smooth shod, and the river frozen half-way over, so we slid around on the ice, and jumped into the icy waters, got wet, crawled out, slid around some more, and finally landed. Mr. Wolf-Voice looked me over, and smilingly

said, "Me think you no like 'em"; wherein his conclu-
sion was eminently correct. Who does like to have a
mass of ice freeze on him when naturally the weather is
cold enough to satisfy a walrus?

It was twelve miles through the defiles of the Bad
Lands to the blue ridge of the high mesa where the
hostiles had lived. The trail was strewn with dead cattle,
some of them having never been touched with a knife.
Here and there a dead pony, ridden to a stand-still
and left nerveless on the trail. No words of mine can
describe these Bad Lands. They are somewhat as Doré
pictured hell. One set of buttes, with cones and mina-
rets, gives place in the next mile to natural freaks of
a different variety, never dreamed of by mortal man. It
is the action of water on clay; there are ashes, or what
looks like them. The painter's whole palette is in one
bluff. A year's study of these colors by Mr. Bierstadt,
Professor Marsh, and Mr. Notman might possibly convey
to the Eastern mind an idea; so we'll amble along after
Mr. Wolf-Voice, and leave that subject intact.

"Hark!" My little party stops suddenly, and we all
listen. I feel stupid.

"You hear 'em?" says Wolf-Voice, in a stage-whisper.

"Hear what?" I say.

"Shots."

Then we all get out our guns and go galloping like mad.
I can't imagine why, but I spur my horse and perform
equestrian feats which in an ordinary frame of mind I
should regard as insane. Down a narrow trail we go, with
the gravel flying, and through a *coulée*, up a little hill, on
top of which we stop to listen, and then away we go.
The blue wall grows nearer, and at last we are under it.
A few cotton-wood trees, some frozen water, a little cleft
on the bluffs, and I see a trail winding upward. I know

these warriors are going up there, but I can't understand precisely how. It is not the first perilous trail I have contemplated; but there are dead cattle lying at the bottom which had fallen off and been killed in the ascent. We dismount and start up. It tells on your wind, and tries the leg muscles. Up a steep place a horse wants to go fast, and you have to keep him from running over you. A bend in the trail where the running water has frozen seems impassable. I jump across it, and then pull the bridle and say, " Come on, boy !" If I were the horse I would balk, but the noble animal will try it. A leap, a plunging, and with a terrible scrabble we are all right. Farther up, and the incline is certainly eighty-five degrees. My horse looses his front feet, but a jerk at the headstall brings him down, and he plunges past me to be caught by an Indian at the top of the trail. For a moment we breathe, and then mount.

Before us is a great flat plain blackened by fire, and with the grass still burning. Away in the distance, in the shimmer of the air waves, are figures.

" Maybe so dey Sioux," says Wolf-Voice. And we gallop towards them.

" What will you do if they are?" I ask.

" Stand 'em off," replies the war-dog.

Half an hour's ride showed them to be some of our Cheyennes. All about the plain were strewn the remains of dead cattle (heads and horns, half-butchered carcasses, and withal a rather impressive smell), coyotes, and ravens —all very like war. These Brulés must have lived well. There were lodge poles, old fires, and a series of rifle pits across the neck of land which the Sioux had proposed to defend; medicine poles, and near them the sacrifices, among which was food dedicated to the Great Spirit, but eventually consumed by the less exalted members of

Casey's command. I vandalized a stone pipe and a rawhide stirrup.

The less curious members of our band had gone south, and Wolf-Voice and I rode along together. We discussed war, and I remember two of Wolf-Voice's opinions. Speaking of infantry and their method of fighting, he said:

"Dese walk-a-heap soldiers dey dig hole—get in—shoot heap—Injun can't do nothin' wid 'em—can't kill 'em—can't do nothin' but jes go 'way."

Then, explaining why the Sioux had shown bad generalship in selecting their position, he turned in his saddle, and said, "De big guns he knock 'em rifle pit, den de calavy lun pas' in column—Injun no stop calavy—kill 'em heap, but no stop 'em—den de walk-a-heap dey come too, and de Sioux dey go ober de bluffs." And with wild enthusiasm he added, "De Sioux dey go to hell!" That prospect seemed to delight Mr. Wolf-Voice immensely.

It was a weary ride over the black and smoking plain. A queer mirage was said by my Indian to be the Cheyenne scouts coming after us. Black figures of animals walking slowly along were "starving bronchos abandoned by the hostiles."

"Cowboy he catch 'em," said Wolf-Voice.

I explained that Colonel Offley had orders not to allow any citizens to cross the Cheyenne River.

"Cowboy he go give um dam ; he come alle samee."

And I thought Wolf-Voice was probably right.

On the southern edge of the bluffs of the mesa we halted, and found water for man and beast. The command gradually concentrated, and for half an hour we stood on the high points scanning the great flats below, and located the dust of the retiring hostile column and

THE HOTCHKISS GUN

the back lying scouts. Lieutenant Casey had positive orders not to bring on an engagement, and only desired to hang on their flanks, so as to keep Miles familiar with the hostile movements. A courier started on his lonely ride back with a note for the major-general. Our scouts were flying about far down the valley, and we filed off after them. Presently a little column of dust follows a flying horseman towards us. On, on he comes. The scouts grow uneasy; wild creatures they are, with the suspicion of a red deer and the stealth of a panther.

The Sioux have fired on our scouts. Off we go at a trot, scattering out, unslinging our guns, and the air full of fight. I ride by Casey, and see he is troubled. The orders in his pocket do not call for a fight. Can he hold these wild warriors?

" Struthers, we have got to hold these men," said Casey, in a tone of voice which was full of meaning. To shorten the story, our men were at last gotten into ranks, and details made to cover the advance. The hostiles were evidently much excited. Little clouds of dust whirling hither and thither showed where the opposing scouts were shadowing each other. The sun was waning, and yet we spurred our weary horses on towards the enemy. Poor beasts! no food and too much exercise since daylight.

The Cheyennes were uneasy, and not at all pleased with this scheme of action. What could they know about the orders in Lieutenant Casey's pocket, prompted by a commanding general thinking of a thousand and one interests, and with telegrams from Washington directing the avoidance of an Indian war?

Old-soldier Thompson even, with all his intelligence and knowledge of things, felt the wild Berserker battle valor, which he smothered with difficulty, and confined

himself to potent remarks and spurring of old Piegan.
He said: "This is a new kind of war. Them Injuns
don't understand it, and to tell you the truth, I don't
nuther. The Injuns say they have come all the way
from Tongue River, and are going back poor. Can't get
Sioux horses, can't kill Sioux," and in peroration he con-
firmed his old impression that "this is a new kind of
war"; and then relapsed into reveries of what things used
to be before General Miles invented this new kind
of war.

In our immediate front was a heavy body of Sioux
scouts. Lieutenant Casey was ahead. Men broke from
our ranks, but were held with difficulty by Struthers and
Getty. Back comes Casey at a gallop. He sees the
crisis, and with his hand on his six - shooter, says, " I will
shoot the first man through the head who falls out of the
ranks." A mutiny is imminent in the Pine Ridge con-
tingent, but the diplomat Struthers brings order at last,
and we file off down the hills to the left, and stop by a
stream, while Casey goes back and meets a body of
Sioux on a high hill for a powwow. I watched through a
glass, and the sun went down as they talked. We had
orders not to remove our saddles, and stood in the line
nervously expecting anything imaginable to happen.
The daring of Casey in this case is simply an instance of
a hundred such, and the last one cost him his life. By
his prompt measures with his own men, and by his courage in going among the Sioux to powwow, he averted a
bloody battle, and obeyed his orders. There was one
man between two banks of savage warriors who were
fairly frothing at the mouth — a soldier; the sun will
never shine upon a better.

At last, after an interminable time, he came away.
Far away to the right are two of our scouts driving two

beeves. We see the bright blaze of the six-shooters, the
steers tumble, and hunger is no longer one of our woes.

The tired horses are unsaddled, to eat and drink and
roll. We lay dry cotton-wood limbs on the fires, heavy
pickets are told off, and our " bull meat " is cooked in the
primitive style. Old Wolf-Voice and another scout are
swinging six ribs on a piece of rawhide over a fire, and
later he brings me a rib and a little bit of coffee from a
roll in his handkerchief. I thought him a " brick," and
mystified him by telling him so.

Three or four Brulés are let in through our pickets, and
come " wagging their tails," as Two-Moons says, but adding, " Don't you trust the Sioux." They protest their
good intentions, borrow tobacco, and say Lieutenant Casey
can send in a wagon for commissaries to Pine Ridge, and
also that I can go through their lines with it. Were
there ever greater liars on earth?

I sat near the fire and looked intently at one human
brute opposite, a perfect animal, so far as I could see.
Never was there a face so replete with human depravity,
stolid, ferocious, arrogant, and all the rest — ghost - shirt,
war-paint, feathers, and arms. As a picture, perfect; as a
reality, horrible. Presently they go away, and we prepare
for the night. This preparing for the night is a rather
simple process. I have stolen my saddle blanket from
my poor horse, and, with this laid on the ground, I try
my saddle in four or five different positions in its capacity
of pillow. The inventor of the Whitman tree never con-
sidered this possible use of his handiwork, or he might
have done better. I next button the lower three buttons
of my overcoat, and thus wrapped " I lie down to pleasant dreams "—of rheumatism.

An hour later and the fires go down. Black forms pass
like uneasy spirits, and presently you find yourself thrash-

ing around in the underbrush across the river after branches to feed that insatiable fire.   One comrade breaks
through the ice and gets wet, and inelegant remarks come
from the shadowy blackness under the river-banks.   I
think a man shouldn't use such language even under such
circumstances, but I also think very few men wouldn't.
A chilling wind now adds to the misery of the situation,
and the heat of the fire goes off in a cloud of sparks to
the No Man's Land across the river.   After smoking a
pipe for two hours your mouth is raw and your nervous
system shattered, so nothing is left but to sit calmly
down and just suffer.   You can hate the Chinese on the
other side of the world, who are now enjoying the rays of
the sun.

And morning finds you in the saddle.   It always does.
I don't know how it is—a habit of life, I suppose.   Morn-
ings ought to find me cosily ensconced in a good bed, but
in retrospect they seem always to be in the saddle, with a
good prospect of all day ahead, and evening finds me with
a chunk of bull meat and without blankets, until one fine
day we come to our wagons, our Sibleys, and the little
luxuries of the mess chest.

The next morning I announced my intention of going
to Pine Ridge Agency, which is twenty-five miles away.
Mr. Thompson, two scouts, and a Swedish teamster are to
go in for provisions and messages.   Mr. Thompson got in
the wagon.   I expressed my astonishment at this and
the fact that he had no carbines, as we expected to go
through the hostile pickets and camp.   He said, "If I
can't talk them Injuns out of killin' me, I reckon I'll have
to go."   I trotted along with Red-Bear and Hairy-Arm,
and a mile and a half ahead went the courier, Wells.
Poor man! in two hours he lay bleeding in the road, with
a bullet through the hips, and called two days for water

before he " struck the long trail to the kingdom come," as the cowboys phrase it.

We could see two black columns of smoke, which we did not understand. After we had gone eight or ten miles, and were just crossing a ravine, we saw a Sioux buck on a little hill just ahead, out of pistol-shot. He immediately rode the " danger signal." Red-Bear turned his horse in the " peace sign," and advanced. – We drove over the ravine, and halted. I dismounted. Six young Brulé Sioux rose out of the ground, and rode up to Red-Bear, and the hills were full of pickets to the right and left. We waited to hear the result of Red-Bear's conversation, when he presently came back and spoke to Thompson in Cheyenne. I looked at him ; his eyes were snapping, and his facial muscles twitched frightfully. This was unusual, and I knew that things were not well.

" Red - Bear says we will have to go back," explained Thompson ; and turning to Red-Bear he requested that two Sioux might come closer, and talk with us. Things looked ominous to me, not understanding Cheyenne, which was being talked. " This is a bad hole, and I reckon our cake is dough right here," said Thompson.

Hairy-Arm's face was impassive, but his dark eyes wandered from Brulé to Brulé with devilish calculation. Two young bucks came up, and one asked Thompson for tobacco, whereat he was handed a package of Durham by Thompson, which was not returned.

" It's lucky for me that tobacco ain't a million dollars," sighed Thompson.

Another little buck slipped up behind me, whereat Mr. Thompson gave me a warning look. Turning, I advanced on him quickly (I wanted to be as near as possible, not being armed), and holding out my hand, said, " How, colah?" He did not like to take it, but he did, and I was saved the trouble of further action.

"We'll never get this wagon turned around," suggested Mr. Thompson, as the teamster whipped up; but we did. And as we commenced our movement on Casey's camp, Mr. Thompson said, "Go slow now; don't run, or they'll sure shoot."

"Gemme gun," said the little scout Red-Bear, and we all got our arms from the wagon.

There was no suspense now. Things had begun to happen. A little faster, yet faster, we go up the little banks of the *coulée*, and, ye gods! what! — five fully armed, well-mounted cowboys — a regular rescue scene from Buffalo Bill's show.

"Go back!" shouted Thompson.

Bang! bang! bang! and the bullets whistle around and kick up the dust. Away we go.

Four bucks start over the hills to our right to flank us. Red-Bear talked loudly in Cheyenne.

Thompson repeated, "Red-Bear says if any one is hit, get off in the grass and lie down; we must all hang together."

We all yelled, "We will."

A well-mounted man rode like mad ahead of the laboring team horses to carry the news to the scout camp. The cowboys, being well mounted, could easily have gotten away, but they stuck like true blues.

Here is where the great beauty of American character comes out. Nothing can be taken seriously by men used to danger. Above the pounding of the horses and the rattle of the wagon and through the dust came the cowboy song from the lips of Mr. Thompson:

"Roll your tail,
And roll her high;

A RUN TO THE SCOUT CAMP

IN THE TRENCHES

We'll all be angels
By-and-by."

We deployed on the flanks of the wagon so that the
team horses might not be shot, which would have stopped
the whole outfit, and we did ten miles at a record-break-
ing gallop. We struck the scout camp in a blaze of excitement. The Cheyennes were in war-paint, and the
ponies' tails were tied up and full of feathers. Had the
Sioux materialized at that time, Mr. Casey would have
had his orders broken right there.

After a lull in the proceedings, Mr. Thompson con-
fided to me that "the next time I go to war in a wagon
it will put the drinks on me"; and he saddled Piegan,
and patted his neck in a way which showed his gratification at the change in transport. We pulled out again
for the lower country, and as our scouts had seen the
dust of Colonel Sanford's command, we presently joined
them.

Any remarks made to Mr. Thompson on the tobacco
subject are taken seriously, and he has intimated to me
a quiet yearning for a shot at "the particular slit-mouthed
Brulé who got away with that Durham."

How we awoke next morning with the sleet freezing
in our faces, and how we made camp in the blizzard, and
borrowed Sibley stoves of the soldiers, and how we were
at last comfortable, and spent New-Year's Eve in a proper manner, is of little interest.

I was awakened at a late hour that night by Captain
Baldwin, of General Miles's staff, and told to saddle up
for a night's ride to Pine Ridge. This was the end of
my experience with Lieutenant Casey and his gallant
corps. We shook hands cheerily in the dim candle-light
of the tepee, and agreeing to meet in New York at some

not distant day, I stepped out from the Sibley, mounted, and rode away in the night.

Three days later I had eaten my breakfast on the dining-car, and had settled down to a cigar and a Chicago morning paper. The big leads at the top of the column said, "Lieutenant E. W. Casey Shot." Casey shot! I look again. Yes; despatches from head-quarters—a fact beyond question.

A nasty little Brulé Sioux had made his *coup*, and shot away the life of a man who would have gained his stars in modern war as naturally as most of his fellows would their eagles. He had shot away the life of an accomplished man; the best friend the Indians had; a man who did not know "fear"; a young man beloved by his comrades, respected by his generals and by the Secretary of War. The squaws of another race will sing the death-song of their benefactor, and woe to the Sioux if the Northern Cheyennes get a chance to *coup !*

"Try to avoid bloodshed," comes over the wires from Washington. "Poor savages!" comes the plaintive wail of the sentimentalist from his place of security; but who is to weep for the men who hold up a row of brass buttons for any hater of the United States to fire a gun at? Are the squaws of another race to do the mourning for American soldiers? Are the men of another race to hope for vengeance? Bah!

I sometimes think Americans lack a virtue which the military races of Europe possess. Possibly they may never need it. I hope not. American soldiers of our frontier days have learned not to expect sympathy in the East, but where one like Casey goes down there are many places where Sorrow will spread her dusky pinions and the light grow dim.

THE SIOUX OUTBREAK IN SOUTH DAKOTA

WE discussed the vague reports of the Wounded Knee fight in the upper camps of the cordon, and old hands said it could be no ordinary affair because of the large casualty. Two days after I rode into the Pine Ridge Agency, very hungry and nearly frozen to death, having ridden with Captain Baldwin, of the staff, and a Mr. Miller all night long. I had to look after a poor horse, and see that he was groomed and fed, which require considerable tact and " hustling " in a busy camp. Then came my breakfast. That struck me as a serious matter at the time. There were wagons and soldiers—the burial party going to the Wounded Knee to do its solemn duty. I wanted to go very much. I stopped to think ; in short, I hesitated, and of course was " lost," for after breakfast they had gone. Why did I not follow them ? Well, my natural prudence had been considerably strengthened a few days previously by a half-hour's interview with six painted Brulé Sioux, who seemed to be in command of the situation. To briefly end the matter, the burial party was fired on, and my confidence in my own good judgment was vindicated to my own satisfaction.

I rode over to the camp of the Seventh United States Cavalry, and met all the officers, both wounded and well, and a great many of the men. They told me their stories in that inimitable way which is studied art with warriors. To appreciate brevity you must go to a sol-

dier. He shrugs his shoulders, and points to the bridge
of his nose, which has had a piece cut out by a bullet,
and says, " Rather close, but don't amount to much."
An inch more, and some youngster would have had his
promotion.

I shall not here tell the story of the Seventh Cavalry
fight with Big Foot's band of Sioux on the Wounded
Knee; that has been done in the daily papers; but I
will recount some small-talk current in the Sibley tepees,
or the "white man's war tents," as the Indians call them.

Lying on his back, with a bullet through the body,
Lieutenant Mann grew stern when he got to the critical
point in his story. " I saw three or four young bucks
drop their blankets, and I saw that they were armed.
' Be ready to fire, men ; there is trouble.' There was an
instant, and then we heard sounds of firing in the centre
of the Indians. ' Fire !' I shouted, and we poured it into
them."

" Oh yes, Mann, but the trouble began when the old
medicine-man threw the dust in the air. That is the old
Indian signal of ' defiance,' and no sooner had he done
that act than those bucks stripped and went into action.
Just before that some one told me that if we didn't stop
that old man's talk he would make trouble. He said that
the white men's bullets would not go through the ghost
shirts."

Said another officer, " The way those Sioux worked
those Winchesters was beautiful." Which criticism, you
can see, was professional.

Added another, " One man was hit early in the firing,
but he continued to pump his Winchester; but growing
weaker and weaker, and sinking down gradually, his shots
went higher and higher, until his last went straight up in
the air."

"Those Indians were plumb crazy. Now, for instance, did you notice that before they fired they raised their arms to heaven? That was devotional."

"Yes, captain, but they got over their devotional mood after the shooting was over," remonstrated a cynic. "When I passed over the field after the fight one young warrior who was near to his death asked me to take him over to the medicine-man's side, that he might die with his knife in the old conjurer's heart. He had seen that the medicine was bad, and his faith in the ghost shirt had vanished. There was no doubt but that every buck there thought that no bullet could touch him."

"Well," said an officer, whose pipe was working into a reflective mood, "there is one thing which I learned, and that is that you can bet that the private soldier in the United States army will fight. He'll fight from the drop of the hat anywhere and in any place, and he'll fight till you call *time*. I never in my life saw Springfield carbines worked so industriously as at that place. I noticed one young fellow, and his gun seemed to just blaze all the while. Poor chap! he's mustered out for good."

I saw the scout who had his nose cut off. He came in to get shaved. His face was covered with strips of court-plaster, and when informed that it would be better for him to forego the pleasure of a shave, he reluctantly consented. He had ridden all day and been in the second day's fight with his nose held on by a few strips of plaster, and he did not see just why he could not be shaved; but after being talked to earnestly by a half-dozen friends he succumbed.

"What became of the man who did that?" I asked of him.

He tapped his Winchester and said, "Oh, I got him all right!"

I went into the hospital tents and saw the poor fellows

lying on the cots, a little pale in the face, and with a
drawn look about the mouth and eyes. That is the serious part of soldiering. No excitement, no crowd of cheer-
ing comrades, no shots and yells and din of battle. A few
watchful doctors and Red Cross stewards with bottles and
bandages, and the grim spectre of the universal enemy
hovering over all, and ready to dart down on any man on
the cots who lay quieter and whose face was more pale
than his fellows.

I saw the Red Cross ambulances draw up in line, and
watched the wounded being loaded into them. I saw
poor Garlington. His blond mustache twitched under
the process of moving, and he looked like a man whose
mustache wouldn't twitch unnecessarily. Lieutenant Hawthorne, who was desperately shot in the groin while working the little Hotchkiss cannon, turned his eyes as they
moved Garlington from the next cot, and then waited patiently for his own turn.

I was talking with old Captain Capron, who commanded the battery at the fight—a grim old fellow, with a red-
lined cape overcoat, and nerve enough for a hundred-ton
gun. He said: "When Hawthorne was shot the gun was
worked by Corporal Weimert, while Private Hertzog carried Hawthorne from the field and then returned to his
gun. The Indians redoubled their fire on the men at the
gun, but it seemed only to inspire the corporal to renewed
efforts. Oh, my battery was well served," continued the
captain, as he put his hands behind his back and looked
far away.

This professional interest in the military process of killing men sometimes rasps a citizen's nerves. To the captain everything else was a side note of little consequence
so long as his guns had been worked to his entire satisfaction. That was the point.

THE ADVANCE GUARD—A MILITARY SACRIFICE

At the mention of the name of Captain Wallace, the
Sibley became so quiet that you could hear the stove
draw and the wind wail about the little canvas town.   It
was always " Poor Wallace!" and " He died like a soldier,
with his empty six-shooter in his right hand, shot through
the body, and with two jagged wounds in his head."

I accosted a soldier who was leaning on a crutch while
he carried a little bundle in his right hand.   " You bet
I'm glad to get out in the sunlight; that old hospital tent
was getting mighty tiresome."

"Where was I shot?"   He pointed to his hip.   "Only
a flesh wound; this is my third wound.   My time is out
in a few days ; but I'm going to re-enlist, and I hope I'll
get back here before this trouble is over.   I want to get
square with these Injuns."   You see, there was considerable human nature in this man's composition.

The ambulance went off down the road, and the burial
party came back.   The dead were for the time forgotten,
and the wounded were left to fight their own battles with
stitches and fevers and suppuration.   The living toiled in
the trenches, or stood out their long term on the pickets,
where the moon looked down on the frosty landscape, and
the cold wind from the north searched for the crevices in
their blankets.

AN OUTPOST OF CIVILIZATION

THE hacienda San José de Bavicora lies northwest from Chihuahua 225 of the longest miles on the map. The miles run up long hills and dive into rocky cañons ; they stretch over never-ending burnt plains, and across the beds of tortuous rivers thick with scorching sand. And there are three ways to make this travel. Some go on foot—which is best, if one has time—like the Tahuramaras ; others take it ponyback, after the Mexican manner ; and persons with no time and a great deal of money go in a coach. At first thought this last would seem to be the best, but the Guerrero stage has never failed to tip over, and the company make you sign away your natural rights, and almost your immortal soul, before they will allow you to embark. So it is not the best way at all, if I may judge from my own experience. We had a coach which seemed to choose the steepest hill on the route, where it then struck a stone, which heaved the coach, pulled out the king-pin, and what I remember of the occurrence is full of sprains and aches and general gloom. Guerrero, too, is only three-fourths of the way to Bavicora, and you can only go there if Don Gilberto, the *patron* of the hacienda—or, if you know him well enough, " Jack "—will take you in the ranch coach.

After bumping over the stones all day for five days, through a blinding dust, we were glad enough when we suddenly came out of the tall timber in the mountain

THE HACIENDA SAN JOSÉ DE BAVICORA

pass and espied the great yellow plain of Bavicora stretch-
ing to the blue hills of the Sierra. In an hour's ride more,
through a chill wind, we were at the ranch. We pulled
up at the entrance, which was garnished by a bunch of
cow-punchers, who regarded us curiously as we pulled our
aching bodies and bandaged limbs from the Concord and
limped into the *patio*.

To us was assigned the room of honor, and after shak-
ing ourselves down on a good bed, with mattress and
sheeting, we recovered our cheerfulness. A hot toddy, a
roaring fireplace, completed the effect. The floor was
strewn with bear and wolf skin rugs ; it had pictures and
draperies on the walls, and in a corner a wash-basin and
pitcher—so rare in these parts—was set on a stand, grand-
ly suggestive of the refinements of luxury we had attained
to. I do not wish to convey the impression that Mexicans do not wash, because there are brooks enough in
Mexico if they want to use them, but wash-basins are the
advance-guards of progress, and we had been on the outposts since leaving Chihuahua.

Jack's man William had been ever-present, and administered to our slightest wish; his cheerful "Good-mo'nin',
gemmen," as he lit the fire, recalled us to life, and after
a rub-down I went out to look at the situation.

Jack's ranch is a great straggling square of mud walls
enclosing two *patios*, with adobe corrals and out-buildings,
all obviously constructed for the purposes of defence. It
was built in 1770 by the Jesuits, and while the English
and Dutch were fighting for the possession of the Mo-
hawk Valley, Bavicora was an outpost of civilization, as
it is to-day. Locked in a strange language, on parchment
stored in vaults in Spain, are the records of this enterprise. In 1840 the good fathers were murdered by the
Apaches, the country devasted and deserted, and the cat-

tle and horses hurried to the mountain lairs of the Apache
devils. The place lay idle and unreclaimed for years,
threatening to crumble back to the dust of which it was
made. Near by are curious mounds on the banks of a
dry *arroyo*. The punchers have dug down into these
ruins, and found adobe walls, mud plasterings, skeletons,
and bits of woven goods. They call them the "Monte-
zumas." All this was to be changed. In 1882 an American cowboy—which was Jack—accompanied by two companions, penetrated south from Arizona, and as he looked
from the mountains over the fair plain of Bavicora, he
said, "I will take this." The Apaches were on every
hand; the country was terrorized to the gates of Chihuahua. The stout heart of the pioneer was not disturbed,
and he made his word good. By purchase he acquired
the plain, and so much more that you could not ride
round it in two weeks. He moved in with his hardy
punchers, and fixed up Bavicora so it would be habitable.
He chased the Indians off his ranch whenever he " cut
their sign." After a while the Mexican *vaqueros* from below overcame their terror, when they saw the American
hold his own with the Apache devils, and by twos and
threes and half-dozens they came up to take service, and
now there are two hundred who lean on Jack and call him
patron. They work for him and they follow him on the
Apache trail, knowing he will never run away, believing
in his beneficence and trusting to his courage.

I sat on a mud - bank and worked away at a sketch
of the yellow sunlit walls of the mud - ranch, with the
great plain running away like the ocean into a violet
streak under the blue line of the Peña Blanca. In the
rear rises a curious broken formation of hills like millions of ruins of Rhine castles. The *lobos** howl by

* Wolves.

EL PATRON

THE ADMINISTRADOR OF SAN JOSÉ DE BAVICORA

night, and the Apache is expected to come at any instant. The old *criada* or serving-woman who makes the beds saw her husband killed at the front door, and every man who goes out of the *patio* has a large assortment of the most improved artillery on his person. Old carts with heavy wooden wheels like millstones stand about. Brown people with big straw hats and gay *serapes* lean lazily against the gray walls. Little pigs carry on the contest with nature, game-chickens strut, and clumsy puppies tumble over each other in joyful play; *burros* stand about sleepily, only indicating life by suggestive movements of their great ears, while at intervals a pony, bearing its lithe rider, steps from the gate, and, breaking into an easy and graceful lope, goes away into the waste of land.

I rose to go inside, and while I gazed I grew exalted in the impression that here, in the year of 1893, I had rediscovered a Fort Laramie after Mr. Parkman's well-known description. The foreman, Tom Bailey, was dressed in store clothes, and our room had bedsteads and a washbasin; otherwise it answered very well. One room was piled high with dried meat, and the great stomachs of oxen filled with tallow; another room is a store full of goods — calicoes, buckskin, *riatas*, yellow leather shoes, guns, and other quaint plunder adapted to the needs of a people who sit on the ground and live on meat and cornmeal.

" Charlie Jim," the Chinese cook, has a big room with a stove in it, and he and the stove are a never-ending wonder to all the folks, and the fame of both has gone across the mountains to Sonora and to the south. Charlie is an autocrat in his curious Chinese way, and by the dignity of his position as Mr. Jack's private cook, and his unknown antecedents, he conjures the Mexicans and damns the

Texans, which latter refuse to take him seriously and kill him, as they would a "proper" man. Charlie Jim, in return, entertains ideas of Texans which he secretes, except when they dine with Jack, when he may be heard to mutter, "Cake and pie no good for puncher, make him fat and lazy"; and when he crosses the *patio* and they fling a rope over his foot, he becomes livid, and breaks out, "Damn puncher; damn rope; rope man all same horse; damn puncher; no good that way."

The *patron* has the state apartment, and no one goes there with his hat on; but the relations with his people are those of a father and children. An old gray man approaches; they touch the left arm with the right—an abbreviated hug; say "Buenos dias, patron!" "Buenos dias, Don Sabino!" and they shake hands. A California saddle stands on a rack by the desk, and the latter is littered with photographs of men in London clothes and women in French dresses, the latter singularly out of character with their surroundings. The old *criada* squats silently by the fireplace, her head enveloped in her blue *rebozo*, and deftly rolls her cigarette. She alone, and one white bull-dog, can come and go without restraint.

The *administrador*, which is Mr. Tom Bailey, of Texas, moves about in the discharge of his responsibilities, and they are universal; anything and everything is his work, from the negotiation for the sale of five thousand head of cattle to the "busting" of a bronco which no one else can "crawl."

The clerk is in the store, with his pink boy's face, a pencil behind his ear, and a big sombrero, trying to look as though he had lived in these wilds longer than at San Francisco, which he finds an impossible part. He has acquired the language and the disregard of time necessary to one who would sell a real's worth of cotton cloth to a Mexican.

The forge in the blacksmith's shop is going, and one puncher is cutting another puncher's hair in the sunlight; ponies are being lugged in on the end of lariats, and thrown down, tied fast, and left in a convulsive heap, ready to be shod at the disposition of their riders.

On the roof of the house are two or three men looking and pointing to the little black specks on the plain far away, which are the cattle going into the *lagunas* to drink.

The second *patio*, or the larger one, is entered by a narrow passage, and here you find horses and saddles and punchers coming and going, saddling and unsaddling their horses, and being bucked about or dragged on a rope. In the little doorways to the rooms of the men stand women in calico dresses and blue cotton *rebozos*, while the dogs and pigs lie about, and little brown *vaqueros* are ripening in the sun. In the rooms you find pottery, stone *metates* for grinding the corn, a fireplace, a symbol of the Catholic Church, some *serapes*, some rope, and buckskin. The people sit on a mat on the floor, and make cigarettes out of native tobacco and corn-husks, or rolled *tortillas;* they laugh and chat in low tones, and altogether occupy the tiniest mental world, hardly larger than the *patio*, and not venturing beyond the little mud town of Temo-zachic, forty miles over the hills. Physically the men vacillate between the most intense excitement and a comatose state of idleness, where all is quiet and slothful, in contrast to the mad whirl of the roaring *rodeo*.

In the haciendas of old Mexico one will find the law and custom of the feudal days. All the laws of Mexico are in protection of the land-owner. The master is without restraint, and the man lives dependent on his caprice. The *patron* of Bavicora, for instance, leases land to a Mexican, and it is one of the arrangements that he shall drive the ranch coach to Chihuahua when it goes. All lessees of land are obliged to follow the *patron* to war, and, indeed, since the common enemy, the Apache, in these parts is as like to harry the little as the great, it is exactly to his interest to wage the war. Then, too, comes the responsibility of the *patron* to his people. He must feed them in the famine, he must arbitrate their disputes, and he must lead them at all times. If through improvidence their work-cattle die or give out, he must restock them, so that they may continue the cultivation of the land, all of which is not altogether profitable in a financial way, as we of the North may think, where all business is done on the "hold you responsible, sir," basis.

The *vaqueros* make their own saddles and *reatas;* only the iron saddle-rings, the rifles, and the knives come from the *patron*, and where he gets them God alone knows, and the puncher never cares. No doctor attends the sick or disabled, old women's nursing standing between life and death. The Creator in His providence has arranged it so that simple folks are rarely sick, and a sprained ankle, a bad bruise from a steer's horn or a pitching horse, are soon remedied by rest and a good constitution. At times instant and awful death overtakes the puncher—a horse in a gopher-hole, a mad steer, a chill with a knife, a blue hole where the .45 went in, a quicksand closing overhead, and a cross on a hill-side are all.

Never is a door closed. Why they were put up I failed to discover. For days I tried faithfully to keep mine shut, but every one coming or going left it open, so that I gave it up in despair. There are only two windows in the ranch of San José de Bavicora, one in our chamber

A HAIR-CUT À LA PUNCHER

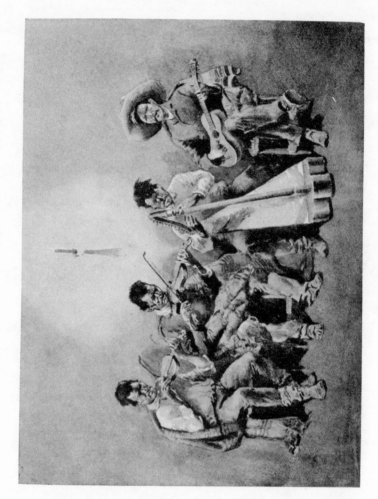

THE MUSIC AT THE "BAILE"

and one in the blacksmith's shop, both opening into the court. In fact, I found those were the only two windows in the state, outside of the big city. The Mexicans find that their enemies are prone to shoot through these apertures, and so they have accustomed themselves to do without them, which is as it should be, since it removes the temptation.

One night the *patron* gave a *baile*. The *vaqueros* all came with their girls, and a string band rendered music with a very dancy swing. I sat in a corner and observed the man who wears the big hat and who throws the rawhide as he cavorted about with his girl, and the way they dug up the dust out of the dirt floor soon put me to coughing. "Candles shed their soft lustre—and tallow" down the backs of our necks, and the band scraped and thrummed away in a most serious manner. One man had a harp, two had primitive fiddles, and one a guitar. One old fiddler was the leader, and as he bowed his head on his instrument I could not keep my eyes off him. He had come from Sonora, and was very old; he looked as though he had had his share of a very rough life; he was never handsome as a boy, I am sure, but the weather and starvation and time had blown him and crumbled him into a ruin which resembled the pre-existing ape from which the races sprang. If he had never committed murder, it was for lack of opportunity; and Sonora is a long travel from Plymouth Rock.

Tom Bailey, the foreman, came round to me, his eyes dancing, and his shock of hair standing up like a Circassian beauty's, and pointing, he said, " Thar's a woman who's prettier than a speckled pup; put your twine on her." Then, as master of ceremonies, he straightened up and sang out over the fiddles and noise: " Dance, thar, you fellers, or you'll git the gout."

In an adjoining room there was a very heavy jug of strong-water, and thither the men repaired to pick up, so that as the night wore on their brains began to whirl after their legs, and they whooped at times in a way to put one's nerves on edge. The band scraped the harder and the dance waxed fast, the spurs clinked, and *bang, bang, bang* went the Winchester rifles in the *patio*, while the chorus "Viva el patron" rang around the room—the Old Guard was in action.

We sat in our room one evening when in filed the *vaqueros* and asked to be allowed to sing for the *patron*. They sat on my bed and on the floor, while we occupied the other; they had their hats in their hands, and their black, dreamy eyes were diverted as though overcome by the magnificence of the apartment. They hemmed and coughed, until finally one man, who was evidently the leader, pulled himself together and began, in a high falsetto, to sing; after two or three words the rest caught on, and they got through the line, when they stopped; thus was one leading and the others following to the end of the line. It was strange, wild music—a sort of general impression of a boys' choir with a wild discordance, each man giving up his soul as he felt moved. The refrain always ended, for want of breath, in a low, expiring howl, leaving the audience in suspense; but quickly they get at it again, and the rise of the tenor chorus continues. The songs are largely about love and women and doves and flowers, in all of which nonsense punchers take only a perfunctory interest in real life.

These are the amusements — although the puncher is always roping for practice, and everything is fair game for his skill; hence dogs, pigs, and men have become as expert in dodging the rope as the *vaqueros* are in throwing it. A mounted man, in passing, will always throw his

rope at one sitting in a doorway, and then try to get away
before he can retaliate by jerking his own rope over his
head. I have seen a man repair to the roof and watch a
doorway through which he expected some comrade to
pass shortly, and watch for an hour to be ready to drop
his noose about his shoulders.

The ranch fare is very limited, and at intervals men are
sent to bring back a steer from the water-holes, which is
dragged to the front door and there slaughtered. A day
of feasting ensues, and the doorways and the gutter-pipes
and the corral fences are festooned with the beef left to
dry in the sun.

There is the serious side of the life. The Apache is an
evil which Mexicans have come to regard as they do the
meteoric hail, the lightning, the drought, and any other
horror not to be averted. They quarrel between themselves over land and stock, and there are a great many
men out in the mountains who are proscribed by the government. Indeed, while we journeyed on the road and
were stopping one night in a little mud town, we were
startled by a fusillade of shots, and in the morning were
informed that two men had been killed the night before,
and various others wounded. At another time a Mexican,
with his followers, had invaded our apartment and expressed a disposition to kill Jack, but he found Jack was
willing to play his game, and gave up the enterprise. On
the ranch the men had discovered some dead stock which
had been killed with a knife. Men were detailed to roam
the country in search of fresh trails of these cattle-killers.
I asked the foreman what would happen in case they
found a trail which could be followed, and he said, " Why,
we would follow it until we came up, and then kill them."
If a man is to "hold down" a big ranch in Northern
Mexico he has got to be "all man," because it is " a

man's job," as Mr. Bailey, of Los Ojos, said — and he knows.

Jack himself is the motive force of the enterprise, and he disturbs the quiet of this waste of sunshine by his presence for about six months in the year. With his strong spirit, the embodiment of generations of pioneers, he faces the Apache, the marauder, the financial risks. He spurs his listless people on to toil, he permeates every detail, he storms, and greater men than he have sworn like troopers under less provocation than he has at times; but he has snatched from the wolf and the Indian the fair land of Bavicora, to make it fruitful to his generation.

There lies the hacienda San José de Bavicora, gray and silent on the great plain, with the mountain standing guard against intruders, and over it the great blue dome of the sky, untroubled by clouds, except little flecks of vapor which stand, lost in immensity, burning bright like opals, as though discouraged from seeking the mountains or the sea whence they came. The marvellous color of the country beckons to the painter; its simple, natural life entrances the blond barbarian, with his fevered brain; and the gaudy *vaquero* and his trappings and his pony are the actors on this noble stage. But one must be appreciative of it all, or he will find a week of rail and a week of stage and a week of horseback all too far for one to travel to see a shadow across the moon.

A RODEO AT LOS OJOS

THE sun beat down on the dry grass, and the punchers were squatting about in groups in front of the straggling log and *adobe* buildings which constituted the outlying ranch of Los Ojos.

Mr. Johnnie Bell, the *capitan* in charge, was walking about in his heavy *chaparras*, a slouch hat, and a white "biled" shirt. He was chewing his long yellow mustache, and gazing across the great plain of Bavicora with set and squinting eyes. He passed us and repassed us, still gazing out, and in his long Texas drawl said, "Thar's them San Miguel fellers."

I looked, but I could not see any San Miguel fellows in the wide expanse of land.

"Hyar, crawl some horses, and we'll go out and meet 'em," continued Mr. Bell; and, suiting the action, we mounted our horses and followed him. After a time I made out tiny specks in the atmospheric wave which rises from the heated land, and in half an hour could plainly make out a cavalcade of horsemen. Presently breaking into a gallop, which movement was imitated by the other party, we bore down upon each other, and only stopped when near enough to shake hands, the half-wild ponies darting about and rearing under the excitement. Greetings were exchanged in Spanish, and the peculiar shoulder tap, or abbreviated embrace, was indulged in. Doubtless a part of our outfit was as strange to Governor Terraza's

men—for he is the *patron* of San Miguel—as they were
to us.

My imagination had never before pictured anything
so wild as these leather-clad *vaqueros*. As they removed
their hats to greet Jack, their unkempt locks blew over
their faces, back off their foreheads, in the greatest disorder. They were clad in terra-cotta buckskin, elaborately
trimmed with white leather, and around their lower legs
wore heavy cowhide as a sort of legging. They were
fully armed, and with their jingling spurs, their flapping
ropes and buckskin strings, and with their gay *scrapes*
tied behind their saddles, they were as impressive a cavalcade of desert-scamperers as it has been my fortune to
see. Slowly we rode back to the corrals, where they dismounted.

Shortly, and unobserved by us until at hand, we heard
the clatter of hoofs, and, leaving in their wake a cloud of
dust, a dozen punchers from another outfit bore down
upon us as we stood under the *ramada* of the ranch-
house, and pulling up with a jerk, which threw the ponies
on their haunches, the men dismounted and approached,
to be welcomed by the master of the *rodeo*.

A few short orders were given, and three mounted men
started down to the springs, and, after charging about, we
could see that they had roped a steer, which they led,
bawling and resisting, to the ranch, where it was quickly
thrown and slaughtered. Turning it on its back, after
the manner of the old buffalo-hunters, it was quickly dis-
robed and cut up into hundreds of small pieces, which is
the method practised by the Mexican butchers, and distributed to the men.

In Mexico it is the custom for the man who gives the
" round-up " to supply fresh beef to the visiting cow-men ;
and on this occasion it seemed that the pigs, chickens, and

COMING TO THE RODEO

WAVING SERAPE TO DRIVE CATTLE

dogs were also embraced in the bounty of the *patron*, for I noticed one piece which hung immediately in front of my quarters had two chickens roosting on the top of it, and a pig and a dog tugging vigorously at the bottom.

The horse herds were moved in from the *llano* and rounded up in the corral, from which the punchers selected their mounts by roping, and as the sun was westering they disappeared, in obedience to orders, to all points of the compass. The men took positions back in the hills and far out on the plain; there, building a little fire, they cook their beef, and, enveloped in their *serapes*, spend the night. At early dawn they converge on the ranch, driving before them such stock as they may.

In the morning we could see from the ranch-house a great semicircle of gray on the yellow plains. It was the thousands of cattle coming to the *rodeo*. In an hour more we could plainly see the cattle, and behind them the *vaqueros* dashing about, waving their *serapes*. Gradually they converged on the *rodeo* ground, and, enveloped in a great cloud of dust and with hollow bellowings, like the low pedals of a great organ, they begin to mill, or turn about a common centre, until gradually quieted by the enveloping cloud of horsemen. The *patron* and the captains of the neighboring ranches, after an exchange of long-winded Spanish formalities, and accompanied by ourselves, rode slowly from the ranch to the herd, and, entering it, passed through and through and around in solemn procession. The cattle part before the horsemen, and the dust rises so as to obscure to unaccustomed eyes all but the silhouettes of the moving thousands. This is an important function in a cow country, since it enables the owners or their men to estimate what numbers of the stock belong to them, to observe the brands, and to inquire as to the condition of the animals and the numbers of calves and "mavericks," and to settle any dispute which may arise therefrom.

All controversy, if there be any, having been adjusted, a part of the punchers move slowly into the herd, while the rest patrol the outside, and hold it. Then a movement soon begins. You see a figure dash at about full speed through an apparently impenetrable mass of cattle; the stock becomes uneasy and moves about, gradually beginning the milling process, but the men select the cattle bearing their brand, and course them through the herd; all becomes confusion, and the cattle simply seek to escape from the ever-recurring horsemen. Here one sees the matchless horsemanship of the punchers. Their little ponies, trained to the business, respond to the slightest pressure. The cattle make every attempt to escape, dodging in and out and crowding among their kind; but right on their quarter, gradually forcing them to the edge of the herd, keeps the puncher, until finally, as a last effort, the cow and the calf rush through the supporting line, when, after a terrific race, she is turned into another herd, and is called "the cut."

One who finds pleasure in action can here see the most surprising manifestations of it. A huge bull, wild with fright, breaks from the herd, with lowered head and whitened eye, and goes charging off indifferent to what or whom he may encounter, with the little pony pattering in his wake. The cattle run at times with nearly the intensity of action of a deer, and whip and spur are applied mercilessly to the little horse. The process of "tailing" is indulged in, although it is a dangerous practice for the man, and reprehensible from its brutality to the cattle. A man will pursue a bull at top speed, will reach over and grasp the tail of the animal, bring it to his saddle, throw his right leg over the tail, and swing his

horse suddenly to the left, which throws the bull rolling
over and over. That this method has its value I have
seen in the case of pursuing "mavericks," where an unsuccessful throw was made with the rope, and the animal
was about to enter the thick timber; it would be impossible to coil the rope again, and an escape would follow but
for the wonderful dexterity of these men in this accom-
plishment. The little calves become separated from their
mothers, and go bleating about; their mothers respond
by bellows, until pandemonium seems to reign. The dust
is blinding, and the puncher becomes grimy and soiled;
the horses lather; and in the excitement the desperate
men do deeds which convince you of their faith that "a
man can't die till his time comes." At times a bull is
found so skilled in these contests that he cannot be dis-
placed from the herd; it is then necessary to rope him
and drag him to the point desired; and I noticed punchers ride behind recalcitrant bulls and, reaching over, spur
them. I also saw two men throw simultaneously for an
immense creature, when, to my great astonishment, he
turned tail over head and rolled on the ground. They
had both sat back on their ropes together.

The whole scene was inspiring to a degree, and well
merited Mr. Yorick's observation that "it is the sport of
kings; the image of war, with twenty-five per cent. of its
danger."

Fresh horses are saddled from time to time, but before
high noon the work is done, and the various "cut-offs" are
herded in different directions. By this time the dust had
risen until lost in the sky above, and as the various bands
of cowboys rode slowly back to the ranch, I observed
their demoralized condition. The economy *per force* of
the Mexican people prompts them to put no more cotton
into a shirt than is absolutely necessary, with the conse-

quence that, in these cases, their shirts had pulled out
from their belts and their *serapes*, and were flapping in
the wind; their mustaches and their hair were perfectly
solid with dust, and one could not tell a bay horse from a
black.

Now come the cigarettes and the broiling of beef. The
bosses were invited to sit at our table, and as the work of
cutting and branding had yet to be done, no time was
taken for ablutions. Opposite me sat a certain individual
who, as he engulfed his food, presented a grimy waste of
visage only broken by the rolling of his eyes and the
snapping of his teeth.

We then proceeded to the corrals, which were made in
stockaded form from gnarled and many-shaped posts set
on an end. The cows and calves were bunched on one
side in fearful expectancy. A fire was built just outside
of the bars, and the branding-irons set on. Into the corrals went the punchers, with their ropes coiled in their
hands. Selecting their victims, they threw their ropes,
and, after pulling and tugging, a bull calf would come out
of the bunch, whereat two men would set upon him and
"rastle" him to the ground. It is a strange mixture of
humor and pathos, this mutilation of calves—humorous
when the calf throws the man, and pathetic when the
man throws the calf. Occasionally an old cow takes an
unusual interest in her offspring, and charges boldly into
their midst. Those men who cannot escape soon enough
throw dust in her eyes, or put their hats over her horns.
And in this case there were some big steers which had
been "cut out" for purposes of work at the plough and
turned in with the young stock; one old grizzled veteran
manifested an interest in the proceedings, and walked
boldly from the bunch, with his head in the air and bellowing; a wild scurry ensued, and hats and *serapes* were

TAILING A BULL

JOHNNIE BELL OF LOS OJOS

thrown to confuse him. But over all this the punchers only laugh, and go at it again. In corral roping they try to catch the calf by the front feet, and in this they become so expert that they rarely miss. As I sat on the fence, one of the foremen, in play, threw and caught my legs as they dangled.

When the work is done and the cattle are again turned into the herd, the men repair to the *casa* and indulge in games and pranks. We had shooting-matches and hundred-yard dashes; but I think no records were broken, since punchers on foot are odd fish. They walk as though they expected every moment to sit down. Their knees work outward, and they have a decided " hitch " in their gait; but once let them get a foot in a stirrup and a grasp on the horn of the saddle, and a dynamite cartridge alone could expel them from their seat. When loping over the plain the puncher is the epitome of equine grace, and if he desires to look behind him he simply shifts his whole body to one side and lets the horse go as he pleases. In the pursuit of cattle at a *rodeo* he leans forward in his saddle, and with his arms elevated to his shoulders he " plugs " in his spurs and makes his pony fairly sail. While going at this tremendous speed he turns his pony almost in his stride, and no matter how a bull may twist and swerve about, he is at his tail as true as a magnet to the pole. The Mexican punchers all use the " ring bit," and it is a fearful contrivance. Their saddle-trees are very short, and as straight and quite as shapeless as a " saw-buck pack-saddle." The horn is as big as a dinner plate, and taken altogether it is inferior to the California tree. It is very hard on horses' backs, and not at all comfortable for a rider who is not accustomed to it.

They all use hemp ropes which are imported from

some of the southern states of the republic, and carry a lariat of hair which they make themselves. They work for from eight to twelve dollars a month in Mexican coin, and live on the most simple diet imaginable. They are mostly *peoned*, or in hopeless debt to their *patrons*, who go after any man who deserts the range and bring him back by force. A puncher buys nothing but his gorgeous buckskin clothes, and his big silver - mounted straw hat, his spurs, his riata, and his *cincha* rings. He makes his *teguas* or buckskin boots, his heavy leggings, his saddle, and the *patron* furnishes his arms. On the round - up, which lasts about half of the year, he is furnished beef, and also kills game. The balance of the year he is kept in an outlying camp to turn stock back on the range. These camps are often the most simple things, consisting of a pack containing his " grub," his saddle, and *serape*, all lying under a tree, which does duty as a house. He carries a flint and steel, and has a piece of sheet-iron for a stove, and a piece of pottery for boiling things in. This part of their lives is passed in a long siesta, and a man of the North who has a local reputation as a lazy man should see a Mexican puncher loaf, in order to comprehend that he could never achieve distinction in the land where *poco tiempo* means forever. Such is the life of the *vaquero*, a brave fellow, a fatalist, with less wants than the pony he rides, a rather thoughtless man, who lacks many virtues, but when he mounts his horse or casts his riata all men must bow and call him master.

The *baile*, the song, the man with the guitar — and under all this *dolce far niente* are their little hates and bickerings, as thin as cigarette smoke and as enduring as time. They reverence their parents, they honor their *patron*, and love their *compadre*. They are grave, and grave even when gay; they eat little, they think less, they meet death calmly, and it's a terrible scoundrel who goes to hell from Mexico.

The Anglo-American foremen are another type entirely. They have all the rude virtues. The intelligence which is never lacking and the perfect courage which never fails are found in such men as Tom Bailey and Johnnie Bell— two Texans who are the superiors of any cow-men I have ever seen. I have seen them chase the "mavericks" at top speed over a country so difficult that a man could hardly pass on foot out of a walk. On one occasion Mr. Bailey, in hot pursuit of a bull, leaped a tremendous fallen log at top speed, and in the next instant "tailed" and threw the bull as it was about to enter the timber. Bell can ride a pony at a gallop while standing up on his saddle, and while Cossacks do this trick they are enabled to accomplish it easily from the superior adaptability of their saddles to the purpose. In my association with these men of the frontier I have come to greatly respect their moral fibre and their character. Modern civilization, in the process of educating men beyond their capacity, often succeeds in vulgarizing them; but these natural men possess minds which, though lacking all embellishment, are chaste and simple, and utterly devoid of a certain flippancy which passes for smartness in situations where life is not so real. The fact that a man bolts his food or uses his table-knife as though it were a deadly weapon counts very little in the game these men play in their lonely range life. They are not complicated, these children of nature, and they never think one thing and say another. Mr. Bell was wont to squat against a fireplace—à la Indian—and dissect the peculiarities of the audience in a most ingenuous way. It never gave offence either, because so guileless. Mr. Bailey, after listen-

ing carefully to a theological tilt, observed that "he believed he'd be religious if he knowed how."

The jokes and pleasantries of the American puncher
are so close to nature often, and so generously veneered
with heart-rending profanity, as to exclude their becoming classic. The cow-men are good friends and virulent
haters, and, if justified in their own minds, would shoot a
man instantly, and regret the necessity, but not the shooting, afterwards.

Among the dry, saturnine faces of the cow punchers
of the Sierra Madre was one which beamed with human
instincts, which seemed to say, "Welcome, stranger!" He
was the first impression my companion and myself had of
Mexico, and as broad as are its plains and as high its
mountains, yet looms up William on a higher pinnacle of
remembrance.

We crawled out of a Pullman in the early morning at
Chihuahua, and fell into the hands of a little black man,
with telescopic pantaloons, a big sombrero with the edges
rolled up, and a grin on his good-humored face like a
yawning *barranca*.

"Is you frens of Mista Jack's?"

"We are."

"Gimme your checks. Come dis way," he said; and
without knowing why we should hand ourselves and our
property over to this uncouth personage, we did it, and
from thence on over the deserts and in the mountains,
while shivering in the snow by night and by day, there
was Jack's man to bandage our wounds, lend us tobacco
when no one else had any, to tuck in our blankets, to
amuse us, to comfort us in distress, to advise and admon-
ish, until the last *adios* were waved from the train as it
again bore us to the border-land.

On our departure from Chihuahua to meet Jack out in

WILLIAM IN ACTION

MOUNTING A WILD ONE

the mountains the stage was overloaded, but a proposition
to leave William behind was beaten on the first ballot; it
was well vindicated, for without William the expedition
would have been a "march from Moscow." There was
only one man in the party with a sort of bass-relief notion
that he could handle the Spanish language, and the relief
was a very slight one—almost imperceptible—the polite-
ness of the people only keeping him from being mobbed.
But William could speak German, English, and Spanish,
separately, or all at once.

William was so black that he would make a dark hole
in the night, and the top of his head was not over four
and a half feet above the soles of his shoes. His legs
were all out of drawing, but forty-five winters had not
passed over him without leaving a mind which, in its
sphere of life, was agile, resourceful, and eminently capable
of grappling with any complication which might arise.
He had personal relations of various kinds with every
man, woman, and child whom we met in Mexico. He
had been thirty years a cook in a cow camp, and could
evolve banquets from the meat on a bull's tail, and was
wont to say, " I don' know so much 'bout dese yar stoves,
but gie me a camp-fire an' I can make de bes' thing yo'
ever threw your lip ober."

When in camp, with his little cast-off English tourist
cap on one side of his head, a short black pipe tipped
at the other angle to balance the effect, and two or three
stripes of white corn-meal across his visage, he would
move round the camp-fire like a cub bear around a huckle-
berry bush, and in a low, authoritative voice have the
Mexicans all in action, one hurrying after water, another
after wood, some making *tortillas*, or cutting up venison,
grinding coffee between two stones, dusting bedding, or
anything else. The British Field-Marshal air was lost in

a second when he addressed " Mister Willie " or " Mister Jack," and no fawning courtier of the Grand Monarch could purr so low.

On our coach ride to Bavicora, William would seem to go up to any ranch-house on the road, when the sun was getting low, and after ten minutes' conversation with the grave Don who owned it, he would turn to us with a wink, and say : " Come right in, gemmen. Dis ranch is yours." Sure enough, it was. Whether he played us for major-generals or governors of states I shall never know, but certainly we were treated as such.

On one occasion William had gotten out to get a hat blown off by the wind, and when he came up to view the wreck of the turn-over of the great Concord coach, and saw the mules going off down the hill with the front wheels, the ground littered with boxes and débris, and the men all lying about, groaning or fainting in agony, William scratched his wool, and with just a suspicion of humor on his face he ventured, " If I'd been hyar, I would be in two places 'fore now, shuah," which was some consolation to William, if not to us.

In Chihuahua we found William was in need of a clean shirt, and we had got one for him in a shop. He had selected one with a power of color enough to make the sun stand still, and with great glass diamonds in it. We admonished him that when he got to the ranch the punchers would take it away from him.

" No, sah ; I'll take it off 'fore I get thar."

William had his commercial instincts developed in a reasonable degree, for he was always trying to trade a silver watch, of the Captain Cuttle kind, with the Mexicans. When asked what time it was, William would look at the sun and then deftly cant the watch around, the hands of which swung like compasses, and he would show you the time within fifteen minutes of right, which little discrepancy could never affect the value of a watch in the land of *mañana*.

That he possessed tact I have shown, for he was the only man at Bavicora whose relations with the *patron* and the smallest, dirtiest Indian "kid," were easy and natural. Jack said of his popularity, "He stands 'way in with the Chinese cook; gets the warm corner behind the stove." He also had courage, for didn't he serve out the ammunition in Texas when his "outfit" was in a life-and-death tussle with the Comanches? did he not hold a starving crowd of Mexican teamsters off the grub-wagon until the boys came back?

There was only one feature of Western life with which William could not assimilate, and that was the horse. He had trusted a bronco too far on some remote occasion, which accounted partially for the kinks in his legs; but after he had recovered fully his health he had pinned his faith to *burros*, and forgotten the glories of the true cavalier.

"No, sah, Mister Jack, I don' care for to ride dat horse. He's a good horse, but I jes hit de flat for a few miles 'fore I rides him," he was wont to say when the cowboys gave themselves over to an irresponsible desire to see a horse kill a man. He would then go about his duties, uttering gulps of suppressed laughter, after the negro manner, safe in the knowledge that the *burro* he affected could "pack his freight."

One morning I was taking a bath out of our wash-basin, and William, who was watching me and the coffee-pot at the same time, observed that "if one of dese people down hyar was to do dat dere, dere'd be a funeral 'fo' twelve o'clock."

William never admitted any social affinity with Mexicans, and as to his own people he was wont to say: "Never have went with people of my own color. Why, you go to Brazos to-day, and dey tell you dere was Bill, he go home come night, an' de balance of 'em be looking troo de grates in de morning." So William lives happily in the "small social puddle," and always reckons to "treat any friends of Mister Jack's right." So if you would know William, you must do it through Jack.

It was on rare occasions that William, as master of ceremonies, committed any indiscretion, but one occurred in the town of Guerrero. We had gotten in rather late, and William was sent about the town to have some one serve supper for us. We were all very busy when William "blew in" with a great sputtering, and said, "Is yous ready for dinner, gemmen?" "Yes, William," we answered, whereat William ran off. After waiting a long time, and being very hungry, we concluded to go and "rustle" for ourselves, since William did not come back and had not told us where he had gone. After we had found and eaten a dinner, William turned up, gloomy and dispirited. We inquired as to his mood. "I do declar', gemmen, I done forget dat you didn't know where I had ordered dat dinner; but dere's de dinner an' nobody to eat it, an' I's got to leave dis town 'fore sunup, pay for it, or die." Unless some one had advanced the money, William's two other alternatives would have been painful.

The romance in William's life even could not be made mournful, but it was the "mos' trouble" he ever had, and it runs like this: Some years since William had saved up four hundred dollars, and he had a girl back in Brazos to whom he had pinned his faith. He had concluded to assume responsibilities, and to create a business in a little

A MODERN SANCHO PANZA

mud town down the big road. He had it arranged to start a travellers' eating-house; he had contracted for a stove and some furniture; and at about that time his dishonest employer had left Mexico for parts unknown, with all his money. The stove and furniture were yet to be paid for, so William entered into hopeless bankruptcy, lost his girl, and then, attaching himself to Jack, he bravely set to again in life's battle. But I was glad to know that he had again conquered, for before I left I overheard a serious conversation between William and the *patron*. William was cleaning a frying-pan by the camp-fire light, and the *patron* was sitting enveloped in his *serape* on the other side.

"Mist' Jack, I's got a girl. She's a Mexican."

"Why, William, how about that girl up in the Brazos?" inquired the *patron*, in surprise.

"Don't care about her now. Got a new girl."

"Well, I suppose you can have her, if you can win her," replied the *patron*.

"Can I, sah? Well, den, I's win her already, sah—dar!" chuckled William.

"Oh! very well, then, William, I will give you a wagon, with two yellow ponies, to go down and get her; but I don't want you to come back to Bavicora with an empty wagon."

"No, sah; I won't, sah," pleasedly responded the lover.

"Does that suit you, then?" asked the *patron*.

"Yes, sah; but, sah, wonder, sah, might I have the two old whites?"

"All right! You can have the two old white ponies;" and, after a pause, "I will give you that old *adobe* up in La Pinta, and two speckled steers; and I don't want you to come down to the ranch except on *baile* nights, and I want you to slide in then just as quiet as any other outsider," said the *patron*, who was testing William's loyalty to the girl.

"All right! I'll do that."

"William, do you know that no true Mexican girl will marry a man who don't know how to ride a charger?" continued the *patron*, after a while.

"Yes; I's been thinking of dat; but dar's dat Timborello, he's a good horse what a man can 'pend on," replied William, as he scoured at the pan in a very wearing way.

"He's yours, William; and now all you have got to do is to win the girl."

After that William was as gay as a robin in the spring; and as I write this I suppose William is riding over the pass in the mountains, sitting on a board across his wagon, with his Mexican bride by his side, singing out between the puffs of his black pipe, "Go on, dar, you muchacos; specks we ever get to Bavicora dis yar gait?"

IN THE SIERRA MADRE WITH THE PUNCHERS

On a chill, black morning the cabins of Los Ojos gave up their inmates at an early hour. The ponies, mules, and *burros* were herded up, and stood shivering in an angle, while about them walked the men, carefully coiling their hair lariats, and watching for an opportunity to jerk them over the heads of the selected ones. The *patron's* black pet walked up to him, but the mounts of my companion and self sneaked about with an evident desire not to participate in the present service. Old *Cokomorachie* and Jim were finally led forth, protesting after the manner of their kind. I carefully adjusted my Whitman's officer-tree over a wealth of saddle blanketing, and slung my Winchester 45-70 and my field-glasses to it. The punchers, both white and brown, and two or three women, regarded my new-fangled saddle with amused glances; indeed, Mr. Bell's Mexican wife laughed at it outright, and Tom Bailey called it "a damn rim-fire." Another humorist thought that "it would give the chickens the pip if they got onto it"; all of which I took good-humoredly, since this was not the first time "your Uncle Samuel" had been away from home; and after some days, when a lot of men were carefully leading sore-backed horses over the mountains, I had cause to remark further on the subject. A Mexican cow-saddle is a double-barrelled affair; it will eat a hole into a horse's spine and a pair of leather breeches

ON THE MOUNTAINS

MY COMRADE

at the same time. If one could ask "Old Jim" about that saddle of mine, I think he would give it an autograph recommend, for he finished the trip with the hide of his back all there.

Leaving the "burro men" to haul and pull at their patient beasts as they bound on their loads, our outfit "pulled out" on what promised to be plenty of travelling. We were to do the rounds of the ranch, explore the mountains, penetrate to the old Apache strongholds, shoot game, find cliff-dwellers' villages, and I expect the dark minds of the punchers hoped for a sight at the ever-burning fire which should discover the lost mine of Tiopa. We were also promised a fight with the "Kid" if we "cut his trail"; and if he "cut ours," we may never live to regret it. Some tame Indians, just in from a hunt in the Rio Chico, had seen three fires, but they had "rolled their tails"* for Bavi-

* Cowboy for travelling rapidly.

cora so promptly that they had not ascertained whether they were Apache or not. The same men we were in the company of had run the "Kid's" band in to the States only two months before, but on our trip that very elusive and very "bad Injun" was not encountered. Much as I should like to see him, I have no regrets, since it is extremely likely that he would have seen me first.

Our little band was composed of the *patron*, Don Gilberto; my travelling companion from New York city, who had never before been west of the Elysian Fields of New Jersey; Bailey and Bell, ranch foremen, and as dauntless spirits as ever the Texas border nurtured; the ranch bookkeeper, a young man "short" on experiences and "long" on hope; Epitacio, an Indian hunter, since outlawed; William, the colored cook; four buckskin Mexican punchers; an old man who was useless for practical purposes, but who was said to be "funny" in Spanish; and two burro men. We were that day to go to the farthest outlying ranch, called the Casa Camadra, and then to stop for a short hunt and to give the punchers time to "gentle" some steers for work-cattle. The puncher method of doing this is beautifully simple, for any animal undergoing this is gentle or dead after it. After scouring the plain for antelope until late, we followed up a creek towards the cabin where we expected to find the punchers and the burro men with their loads of creature comforts, and as we rode in it was raining a cold sleet. The little log-cabin was low, small, and wonderfully picturesque. It was a typical "shack," such as one used to see in the Northwest when the hunters were there. Out in the rain sat two punchers, enveloped in their *serapes*, engaged in watching a half-dozen big steers eat grass. Inside of the cabin was William by a good fire in a most original fireplace, glowing with heat and pride over his corn-cakes and "marrow-gut." Between various cigarettes, the last drink of *tequela*, and the drying of our clothes, we passed the time until William had put the "grub" on a pack - saddle blanket and said, "Now, gemmen, fly in."

"Fly in" is vulgar, but it is also literal, for we did that: we did not dine—we flew in. The expression and the food were both good. Outside, the cold rain had turned into a wet snow, and we all crowded into the little place and squatted or lay about on the floor. With fingers and hunting-knives we carved and tore at the mountain of beef. The punchers consume enormous quantities of meat, and when satiated they bring forth their corn-husks and tobacco-pouches, and roll their long, thin cigarettes, which burn until they draw their *serapes* about their heads and sink back in dreamless sleep. It is all beautifully primitive, and as I rise on my elbow to look across the blanketed forms packed like mackerel in a cask, to hear their heavy breathing, and see the fire glow, and hear the wind howl outside, I think how little it takes to make men happy. Tom Bailey and Johnnie Bell, the ranch foremen, had faces which would have been in character under a steel head-piece at Cressy, while the wildest blood of Spain, Morocco, and the American Indian ran in the veins of the punchers; and all these men were untainted by the enfeebling influences of luxury and modern life. A chunk of beef, a cigarette, an enveloping *serape*, with the Sierras for a bedroom, were the utmost of their needs.

The sunlight streamed down the big chimney, and William's "Good-mo'nin', sah," brought back my senses. Beyond his silhouette, as he crouched before the fireplace, I could hear the sputtering of the broiling steak. I repaired to the brook and smashed the ice for a rub-down. It was still drizzling, and the landscape lay under a heavy fog.

SHOOTING IN THE SIERRA MADRE

Outside the cabin lay the dead body of a skinned wolf, and about a small fire crouched the punchers.

Breakfast over, the men rode off by twos into the fog, and as Tom Bailey and I jogged along together we reasoned that if we were to strike the point of the mountains and then keep well in the timber we might catch a bunch of antelope which we had "jumped" the day before on the plain below. So all day long we rode over the wet rocks, under the drip and drizzle of the mountain pines, up hill and down dale, and never "cut a sign." It was our luck; for on riding up to the "shack" we saw the bodies of deer, antelope, a big gray wolf, and the skin of a mountain-lion. We were requested to view the game, and encouraged to comment on it; but Tom and I sought a dark corner of the cabin to consume our coffee and cigarettes in silence.

At the Casa Camadra are two other log-houses, and in them live some squalid, yellow-hided humans who are to farm a little stretch of bottom-land this year. They require work-steers to do their ploughing, and Mr. Bell has brought up half a dozen vicious old "stags," which are both truculent and swift of foot. The Mexicans insist that they are not able to handle them; and Mr. Bell orders his punchers into action. I strolled out to the corrals to see the bulls "gentled." After a lot of riding and yelling they were herded and dragged into the enclosure, where they huddled while seven punchers sat on their ponies at the gate. I was standing at one corner of the corral, near the men, when out from the midst of the steers walked a big black bull, which raised its head and gazed directly at me. The bull had never before in his stupid life observed a man on foot, and I comprehended immediately what he would do next, so I "led out" for the casa at a rate of speed which the boys afterwards never grew weary of commending. No spangled *torero* of the bull-ring ever put more heart and soul into his running than did I in my great-coat and long hunting-spurs. The bull made a "fo'lorn hope" for the gate, and the gallant punchers melted away before the charge.

The diversion of the punchers made the retreat of the infantry possible, and from an intrenched position I saw the bulls tear over the hill, with the punchers "rolling their tails" behind. After an hour of swearing and hauling and bellowing, the six cattle were lugged back to the pen, and the bars put up. The punchers came around to congratulate me on my rapid recovery from a sprained ankle, when they happened to observe the cattle again scouring off for the open country. Then there was a grunting of ponies as the spurs went in, some hoarse oaths, and for a third time they tore away after the "gentle work-oxen." The steers had taken the bars in their stride. Another hour's chase, and this time the animals were thrown down, trussed up like turkeys for the baking, and tied to posts, where they lay to kick and bellow the night through in impotent rage. The punchers coiled their ropes, lit their cigarettes, and rode off in the gathering gloom. The morning following the steers were let up, and though wet and chilled, they still roared defiance. For agricultural purposes a Mexican "stag" would be as valuable as a rhinoceros or a Bengal tiger, and I await with interest the report of the death-rate at the Casa Camadra during spring ploughing.

In the handling of these savage animals the punchers are brave to recklessness, but this is partly because it seems so. In reality they have a thorough knowledge of bull nature, and can tell when and where he is going to strike as quickly as a boxer who knows by the "skim on the eye" of his opponent. But still they go boldly into the corral with the maddened brutes, seeming to pay no heed to the imminent possibilities of a trip to the moon. They toss their ropes and catch the bull's feet, they skilfully avoid his rush, and in a spirit of bravado they touch the horns, pat him on the back, or twist his tail.

After hunting for another day, with more success, we packed up and "pulled out" up the Varras Creek towards the mountains, leaving the last house behind us. Beyond was the unknown country. For many miles it had been ridden by some of the punchers, but the country is large, covered with vast mountain ranges, with wastes of stony foot-hills at the bases, while *barrancas* yawn at your feet, and for a great many years the policy of the Apaches has been not to encourage immigration. In 1860 a heavy band of Mexican prospectors undertook to penetrate this part in the quest of Tiopa, but they were driven out. It is now possible for strong outfits to travel its wilds with only a small chance of encountering Apache renegades, but very few have attempted it as yet. It is so remote that prospectors for silver or gold could hardly work a mine if they found one, and for other purposes it has little value. The most magnificent pine timber covers its slopes, but it would take a syndicate to deliver one log at the railroad. As we wound our way up the Varras Creek we passed beetling crags and huge pillars of porphyry rock cut into fantastic shapes by water and frost, resplendent in color, and admirably adapted for the pot-hunting of humans as affected by gentry temporarily stopping at San Carlos.

In a dell in the forest we espied some "mavericks," or unbranded stock. The punchers are ever alert for a beef without half its ears gone and a big HF burned in its flank, and immediately they perceive one they tighten their *cincha*, slip the rope from the pommel, put their hats on the back of their heads, and "light out." A cow was soon caught, after desperate riding over rocks and fallen timber, thrown down, and " hog-tied," which means all four feet together. A little fire is built, and one side of a *cincha* ring is heated red-hot, with which a rawhide artist paints HF in the sizzling flesh, while the cow kicks and bawls. She is then unbound, and when she gets back on her feet the *vaqueros* stand about, *serape* in hand, after the bull-fighter method, and provoke her to charge. She charges, while they avoid her by agile springs and a flaunting of their rags. They laugh, and cry " Bravo toro!" until she, having overcome her indignation at their rudeness, sets off down the cañon with her tail in the air.

Thus we journeyed day by day over the hills and up the cañons, camping by night under the pines in mountain glades or deep ravines, where the sun sets at four o'clock, while it is light above. The moon was in the full and the nights were frosty, and many times we awoke to think it morning when only our heads had become uncovered by the blankets and the big white moon shone fair upon us. Getting up in the night to poke the fire and thaw the stiffening out of one's legs is called by the boys "playing freeze-out," and we all participate in the game. A cigarette at two o'clock in the morning, with one's back to the fire, while the moon looks down on you, your comrades breathing about you, a wolf howling mournfully from a neighboring hill, the mountains towering on every side, and the tall pines painting inky shadows across the ghostly grass, is a mild sensation and rather pleasant. Some of the men are on foot, from soring their horses' backs, and their buckskin boots are wearing out, so they sit about the fire and stitch. We are all very dirty, and I no longer take comfort in watching the cook

THE CLIFF-DWELLINGS

who makes the bread, for fear I may be tempted to ask
him if he will not wash his hands, whereat the boys may
indicate that I am a " dude," and will look down on me.
The flour is nearly gone, and shortly it will not matter
whether the cook's hands are rusty or not.   The coffee
and sugar promise to hold out.   When William can no
longer serve " bull gravy " with his fried meat I shall have
many regrets, but they are swamped by the probabilities
of a tobacco famine, which is imminent.   We get deer
every day, but to one not used to a strictly meat diet it
begins to pall.   The Indian hunter takes the stomach of
a deer, fills it with meat, and deposits it under the coals.
We roast it in slices and chunks, but I like it better when
" jerked " brown, as it then affords somewhat more mystery to a taste already jaded with venison.   In travelling
with pack - animals it is the custom to make a day's
march before halting, and a day's march ends about four
o'clock, or when water is found.   Ten hours' march will
loosen one's cartridge-belt five or six holes, for venison
and coffee is not a strong food.   By 12 M. we acquire a
wolfish yearning for the " flesh-pots," but that shortly is
relieved by the contraction of the stomach, or three or
four quarts of mountain water will afford some relief.   By
nightfall one can " fly into " a venison steak, while cigarettes, coffee, and a desire to lie down restore one's equa-
nimity.

We have passed some small ranges and worm our way
down bottomless pits, but at last there rises ahead the
main range of the Sierra Madre.   From the depths of a
great *barranca* we begin the climb.   Never have I seen
hills as sideling as these.   It is terrible work for one not
used to mountain-climbing and the short allowance of air
one finds to subsist on.   The feeling of exhaustion is almost impossible to overcome.   The horses are thin, and

Old Jim is developing more ribs than good condition calls for, so I walk to ease the old fellow. There are snow fields to cross, which intensifies the action. The journey is enlivened at times by shots at deer, and the rifles echo around the mountains, but being long shots they are misses. We passed the *cordon* of the mountains, and stopped on a knife-like ridge where the melting snows under one's foot ran east and west to the two great oceans. The climb from here over the main range was a bellows-bursting affair, but as we pulled on to the high *mesa* our drooping nerves were stiffened by shots, and presently deer came bounding down the ravine to our left. Jack made a bully flying shot, and the stricken deer rolled many yards, until caught by a fallen log. My companion, who was in advance, had fired into some deer, and had shot a buck which was lying down, and he was much puffed up with pride over this achievement in still-hunting. From there on we passed through the most wonderful natural deer park. The animals did not fear man, and stood to be fired at, though the open timber and absence of underbrush made the shots long-range ones. After killing all we could carry, we sat down to wait for the *burro* train.

That night we camped on a jutting crag, with the water running in the *barranca* two hundred feet below us. For a hundred miles the mountain and plain lay at our feet —a place more for an eagle's eyrie than a camp for a caravan. The night set very cold, and from out in space the moon threw its mellow light down upon us. Before the camp-fire our Indian hunter told the story of the killing of Victoria's band, where he had been among the victors, and as he threw his *serape* down, and standing forth with the firelight playing on his harsh features, he swayed his body and waved his hands, while with hoarse voice and

in a strange language he gave the movement of the fight.
The legend of the lost mine of Tiopa was narrated by a
vaquero in the quiet manner of one whose memory goes
far back, and to whom it is all real—about the Jesuits,
the iron door over the mouth of the mine, its richness,
the secrecy enjoined by the fathers on the people when
they fled before the Apache devils, and how there is always a light to be kept burning at its entrance to guide
them back.   It was a grand theatre and an eerie scene.

On the other side of the mountain we found the trail
most difficult.   I would never have believed that a horse
could traverse it.   To say that it was steep is common-
place, and yet I cannot be believed if I say that it was
perpendicular; but a man could toss his hat a mile at
any moment if he pleased.   Then, underfoot, it was all
loose lava rock, and the little ponies had to jump and
dance over the bowlders.   When we had finally arrived on
a grassy *mesa* I concluded that if ever again I did the like
of that, it would most certainly be the result of a tremendous error in my calculations.   The pack-train was here
detached and sent to water, but we followed Jack to see
his " discovery."   After miles of travel through the dry,
yellow grass we came out on a high bluff with a *barranca*
at its foot, the bottom of which we could not see.   On
the overhanging wall opposite were Jack's cliff-dwellings,
perched like dove-cots against the precipice.   It was only
a quarter of a mile to them, but it took two days to get
there, so we did not go.   There are also holes in the cliffs,
and underground passages.   The paths up to them are
washed away, but Jack and some of his men have invaded the silent village.   They climbed up with lariats, and
he was let down over the cliff, but they found nothing
left but dust and cobwebs.

We could not get down to water, and as our horses

were thirsty and foot-sore, we "mogged along." On our ride we " cut the trail " of a big band of mustangs, or wild horses, but did not see them, and by late afternoon we found the camp, and William busy above his fire. After hunting down the valley for a few days for " burro deer " and wild turkey, we found that the tobacco was promptly giving out, according to calculations, and, being all invet- erate smokers, we "made trail fast " for the Neuearachie ranch. Our ponies were jaded and sore ; but having " roped " a stray pony two days before, which was now fresh, the lightest *vaquero* was put on his back, and sent hot-foot in the night to the ranch for tobacco. He made the long ride and returned at noon the next day on a fresh mount, having been thirty-six hours in the saddle. This fellow was a rather remarkable man, as it was he who, on the beginning of the trip, had brought some im- portant mail to us one hundred and seventy miles, and after riding down two ponies he followed our trail on foot through the mountains, and overtook us as we sat resting on a log in the woods.

How we at last pulled into the ranch at Neuearachie, with its log buildings and irrigated fields, and how we "swooped down " on Mr. John Bailey, and ate up all his eggs and bread and butter at the first onset, I will not weary you with, but I believe that a man should for one month of the year live on the roots of the grass, in order to understand for the eleven following that so-called ne- cessities are luxuries in reality. Not that I would indis- criminately recommend such a dietary abasement as ours, yet will I insist that it has killed less men than gluttony, and should you ever make the Sierra trails with the punchers, you will get rather less than more.

BLACK WATER AND SHALLOWS

THE morning broke gray and lowering, and the clouds rolled in heavy masses across the sky. I was sitting out on a log washing a shirt, and not distinguishing myself as a laundryman either, for one shirt will become excessively dirty in a week, and no canoeist can have more than that, as will be seen when you consider that he has to carry everything which he owns on his back. My guide had packed up our little "kit" and deposited it skilfully in the *Necoochee* — a sixteen-foot canoe of the Rice Lake pattern.

We were about to start on a cruise down a river which the lumbermen said could not be "run," as it was shallow and rocky. We could find no one who had been down it, and so, not knowing anything about it, we regarded it as a pleasant prospect. "Harrison," being a professional guide and hunter, had mostly come in contact with people — or "sports," as he called them — who had no sooner entered the woods than they were overcome with a desire to slay. No fatigue or exertion was too great when the grand purpose was to kill the deer and despoil the trout streams, but to go wandering aimlessly down a stream which by general consent was impracticable for boats, and then out into the clearings where the mountain-spring was left behind, and where logs and mill-dams and agriculturists took the place of the deer and the trout, was a scheme which never quite got straightened out in his mind. With many misgivings, and a very clear impression that I was mentally deranged, "Has" allowed that "we're all aboard."

We pushed out into the big lake and paddled. As we skirted the shores the wind howled through the giant hemlocks, and the ripples ran away into white-caps on the far shore. As I wielded my double-blade paddle and instinctively enjoyed the wildness of the day, I also indulged in a conscious calculation of how long it would take my shirt to dry on my back. It is such a pity to mix a damp shirt up with the wild storm, as it hurries over the dark woods and the black water, that I felt misgivings; but, to be perfectly accurate, they divided my attention, and, after all, man is only noble by fits and starts.

We soon reached the head of the river, and a water-storage dam and a mile of impassable rapids made a "carry" or "portage" necessary. Slinging our packs and taking the seventy-pound canoe on our shoulders, we started down the trail. The torture of this sort of thing is as exquisitely perfect in its way as any ever devised. A trunk-porter in a summer hotel simply does for a few seconds what we do by the hour, and as for reconciling this to an idea of physical enjoyment, it cannot be done. It's a subtle mental process altogether indefinable; but your enthusiast is a person who would lose all if he reasoned any, and to suffer like an anchorite is always a part of a sportsman's programme. The person who tilts back in a chair on the veranda of a summer hotel, while he smokes cigars and gazes vacantly into space, is your only true philosopher; but he is not a sportsman. The woods and the fields and the broad roll of the ocean do not beckon to him to come out among them. He detests all their sensations, and believes nothing holy except the

THE PORTAGE.

BLACK WATER

dinner-hour, and with his bad appetite that too is flat, stale, and unprofitable. A real sportsman, of the nature-loving type, must go tramping or paddling or riding about over the waste places of the earth, with his dinner in his pocket. He is alive to the terrible strain of the " carry," and to the quiet pipe when the day is done. The camp-fire contemplation, the beautiful quiet of the misty morning on the still water, enrapture him, and his eye dilates, his nerves tingle, and he is in a conflagration of ecstasy. When he is going—going—faster—faster into the boil of the waters, he hears the roar and boom ahead, and the black rocks crop up in thickening masses to dispute his way. He is fighting a game battle with the elements, and they are remorseless. He may break his leg or lose his life in the tip-over which is imminent, but the fool is happy—let him die.

But we were left on the " carry," and it is with a little thrill of joy and the largest sigh of relief possible when we again settle the boat in the water. Now you should understand why it is better to have one shirt and wash it often. My " canoe kit " is the best arranged and the most perfect in the world, as no other canoeist will possibly admit, but which is nevertheless a fact. One blanket, a light shelter-tent, a cooking outfit, which folds up in a sort of Japanese way, a light axe, two canvas packs, and tea, bacon, and flour. This does not make long reading, but it makes a load for a man when it's all packed up, and a canoeist's baggage must be cut to the strength of his back. It is a great piece of confidence in which I will indulge you when I caution you not to pick out invalids for canoe companions. If a *burro* would take kindly to backwoods navigation, I should enjoy the society of one, though it would not be in the nature of a *burro* to swing an axe, as indeed there are many fine gentlemen who can-

not do a good job at that; and if one at least of the party
cannot, the camp-fires will go out early at nights, and it
is more than probable that the companions will have less
than twenty toes between them at the end of the cruise.

All these arrangements being perfected, you are ready
to go ahead, and in the wilderness you have only one
anxiety, and that is about the "grub." If the canoe turn
over, the tea, the sugar, and the flour will mix up with the
surrounding elements, and only the bacon will remain to
nourish you until you strike the clearings, and there are
few men this side 70° north latitude who will gormandize
on that alone.

The long still water is the mental side of canoeing, as
the rapid is the life and movement. The dark woods
tower on either side, and the clear banks, full to their fat
sides, fringed with trailing vines and drooping ferns, have
not the impoverished look of civilized rivers. The dark
water wells along, and the branches droop to kiss it. In
front the gray sky is answered back by the water reflection, and the trees lie out as though hung in the air, forming a gateway, always receding. Here and there an old
monarch of the forest has succumbed to the last blow and
fallen across the stream. It reaches out ever so far with
its giant stems, and the first branch had started sixty
feet from the ground. You may have to chop a way
through, or you may force your canoe through the limbs
and gather a crowd of little broken branches to escort
you along the stream. The original forest tree has a
character all its own, and I never see one but I think of
the artist who drew second-growth timber and called it
"the forest primeval." The quietness of the woods, with
all their solemnity, permitting no bright or overdressed
plant to obtrude itself, is rudely shocked by the garish
painted thing as the yellow polished *Necoochee* glides

among them. The water-rat dives with a tremendous splash as he sees the big monster glide by his sedge home. The kingfisher springs away from his perch on the dead top with loud chatterings when we glide into his notice. The crane takes off from his grassy "set back" in a deliberate manner, as though embarking on a tour to Japan, a thing not to be hurriedly done. The mink eyes you from his sunken log, and, grinning in his most savage little manner, leaps away. These have all been disturbed in their wild homes as they were about to lunch off the handiest trout, and no doubt they hate us in their liveliest manner; but the poor trout under the boat compensate us with their thanks. The mud-turtle is making his way up-stream, as we can tell by the row of bubbles which arise in his wake; and the "skaters," as I call the little insects which go skipping about like a lawyer's point in an argument, part as we go by. The mosquitoes, those desperate little villains who dispute your happiness in the woods, are there, but they smell the tar and oil of our war-paint, and can only hum in their anger. A stick cracks in the brush, and with all the dash and confidence of a city girl as she steps from her front door, a little spotted fawn walks out on a sedge bank from among the alders. He does not notice us, but in his stupid little way looks out the freshest water-grass, and the hunter in the stern of the boat cuts his paddle through the water, and the canoe glides silently up until right under his nose. We are still and silent. The little thing raises its head and looks us full in the eye, and then continues to feed as before. I talk to him quietly, and say, " Little man, do not come near the ponds or the rivers, for you will not live to have five prongs on your antlers if any one but such good people as we see you." He looks up, and seems to say, "You are noisy, but I do not care."

"Now run; and if you ever see anything in the forest
which resembles us, run for your life"; and with a bound
the little innocent has regained the dark aisles of the
woods. You loll back on your pack, your pipe going

THE FAWN

lazily; your hat is off; you moralize, and think thoughts
which have dignity. You drink in the spell of the forest,
and dream of the birch barks and the red warriors who
did the same thing a couple of centuries since. But as
thoughts vary so much in individuals, and have but an

BREAKING A JAM.

HUNG UP

indirect bearing on canoeing, I will proceed without them. The low swamp, with its soft timber, gives place to hills and beech ridges, and the old lord of the forest for these last hundred years towers up majestically. The smaller trees fight for the sunlight, and thus the ceaseless war of nature goes on quietly, silently, and alone. The miserable "witch-hoppel" leads its lusty plebeian life, satisfied to spring its half-dozen leaves, and not dreaming to some day become an oak. The gentle sigh of the forest, the hum of insects, and the chatter and peal of the birds have gone into harmony with a long, deep, swelling sound, becoming louder and louder, until finally it drowns all else.

The canoe now glides more rapidly. The pipe is laid one side. The paddle is grasped firmly, and with a firm eye I regard the "grub" pack which sits up in the bow, and resolve to die if necessary in order that it may not sink if we turn over. The river turns, and the ominous growl of the rapids is at hand.

"Hold her—hold her now—to the right of the big rock; then swing to the far shore : if we go to the right, we are gone."

"All right; let her stern come round," and we drop away.

No talking now, but with every nerve and muscle tense, and your eye on the boil of the water, you rush along. You back water and paddle, the stern swings, she hangs for an instant, she falls in the current, and with a mad rush you take it like a hunting-man a six-bar gate. Now paddle, paddle, paddle. It looks bad—we cannot make it—yes—all right, and we are on the far shore, with the shallows on the other side. This little episode was successful, but, as you well know, it cannot last. The next rift, and with a bump she is hung upon a sunken rock, and—jump! jump!—we both flounder overboard in any way possible, so it is well and quickly done. One man loses his hold, the other swings the boat off, and, kicking and splashing for a foothold, the demoralized outfit shoots along. At last one is found, and then at a favorable rock we embark again.

You are now wet, but the tea and sugar are safe, so it's a small matter. A jam of logs and tops is "hung up" on a particularly nasty place, and you have a time getting the boat around it. You walk on rotten tops while the knots stick up beneath you like sabres. "Has" floats calmly out to sea, as it were, on a detached log which he is cutting, and with a hopeless look of despair he totters, while I yell, "Save the axe, —— you—save the axe!" and over he goes, only to get wet and very disgusted, both of which will wear off in time. For a mile the water is so shallow that the boat will not run loaded, and we lead her along as we wade, now falling in over our heads, sliding on slippery stones, hurting our feet, wondering why we had come at all. The boat gets loose, and my heart stands still as the whole boat-load of blankets and grub with our pipes and tobacco started off for the settlements —or "drifting to thunder," as Bret Harte said of Chiquita. There was rather a lively and enthusiastic pursuit instituted then, the details of which are forgotten, as my mind was focussed on the grub-pack, but we got her. About this time the soles let go on my tennis shoes, and my only pair of trousers gave way. These things, however, become such mere details as to be scarcely noticed when you have travelled since sunrise up to your waist in water, and are tired, footsore, and hungry. It is time to go ashore and camp.

You scrape away a rod square of dirt, chunks, witchhoppel, and dead leaves, and make a fire. You dry your clothes while you wear the blanket and the guide the shelter - tent, and to a casual observer it would look as though the savage had come again; but he would detect a difference, because a white man in a blanket is about as inspiring a sight as an Indian with a plug-hat.

Finally the coffee boils, the tent is up, and the bough bed laid down. You lean against the dead log and swap lies with the guide; and the greatest hunters I have ever known have all been magnificent liars. The two go together. I should suspect a man who was deficient. Since no one ever believes hunters' yarns, it has come to be a pleasurable pastime, in which a man who has not hunted considerably can't lie properly without offending the intelligence of that part of his audience who have.

The morning comes too soon, and after you are packed up and the boat loaded, if you are in a bad part of the river you do this: you put away your pipe, and with a grimace and a shudder you step out into the river up to your neck and get wet. The morning is cold, and I, for one, would not allow a man who was perfectly dry to get into my boat, for fear he might have some trepidation about getting out promptly if the boat was "hung up" on a rock; and in the woods all nature is subservient to the "grub."

Hour after hour we waded along. A few rods of still water and "Has" would cut off large chews of tobacco, and become wonderfully cynical as to the caprices of the river. The still water ends around the next point. You charge the thing nobly, but end up in the water up to your neck with the "grub" safe, and a mile or so more of wading in prospect.

Then the river narrows, and goes tumbling off down a dark cañon cut through the rocks. We go ashore and "scout the place," and then begin to let the boat down on a line. We hug the black sides like ants, while the water goes to soapsuds at our feet. The boat bobs and rocks, and is nearly upset in a place where we cannot follow it through. We must take it up a ledge about thirty feet high, and after puffing and blowing and feats of maniacal strength, we at last have it again in the water. After some days of this thing we found from a statistician we had dropped 1100 feet in about fifty-one miles, and with the well-known propensity of water to flow downhill, it can be seen that difficulties were encountered. You cannot carry a boat in the forest, and you will discover enough reasons why in a five-minute trail to make their enumeration tiresome. The zest of the whole thing lies in not knowing the difficulties beforehand, and then, if properly equipped, a man who sits at a desk the year through can find no happier days than he will in his canoe when the still waters run through the dark forests and the rapid boils below.

COACHING IN CHIHUAHUA

THAT coaching is a grand sport I cannot deny, for I know almost nothing of it beyond an impression that there is a tremendous amount of mystery connected with its rites. As a sport I have never participated in it, but while travelling the waste places of the earth I have used it as a means on occasion. I never will again. There is no place to which I desire to go badly enough to go in a coach, and such points of interest as are inaccessible except by coach are off my trail. I am not in the least superstitious, and am prone to scout such tendencies; but I'm a Jonah in a stage-coach, and that is not a superstition, but a fact amply proven by many trials. I remember as a boy in Montana having been so hopelessly mixed up with a sage-bush on a dark night when the stage overturned that it left an impression on me. Later in life I was travelling in Arizona, and we were bowling along about ten miles an hour down a great "hog-back" to the plains below. A "swing mule" tripped up a "lead mule," and the stage—with myself on the box—ran over the whole six, and when the driver and I separated ourselves from the mules, shreds of harness, splinters, hair, hide, cargo, and cactus plants I began to formulate the intelligence that stage-coaching was dangerous.

While riding in an army ambulance with Major Viele, of the First Cavalry, and the late Lieutenant Clark, of the Tenth, the brake-beam broke on the descent of a hill,

and we only hit the ground in the high places for about a
mile.   I will not insist that every man can hold his breath
for five consecutive minutes, but I did it.   Thereupon I
formulated vows and pledges.   But like the weak creature
I am, I ignored all this and got into one at Chihuahua last
winter, and first and last did five hundred miles of jolting,
with all the incident and the regulation accident which

A COACHERO

THE START

MORNING TOILET

goes to make up that sort of thing. Now I like to think that I have been through it all, and am alive and un-maimed; and I take a great deal of comfort in knowing that, however I may meet my end, a stage-coach will be in no way connected with it.

On the trip out we had mules. They were black and diminutive. To me a Mexican mule seems to be the Chinaman of the dumb animals. They are enduring beyond comprehension, and they have minds which are patient, yet alert and full of guile. The Mexican *coach-eros* have their mules trained, as bankers do their depositors in our land. They back up against a wall and stand in line while one by one they are harnessed. In the early morning I liked to see the lantern-light glorify the little black creatures against the adobe wall, and hear the big *coachero* talk to his beasts in that easy, familiar way and with that mutual comprehension which is lost to those of the human race who have progressed beyond the natural state. This coachman was an enormous man—big, bony, and with Sullivanesque shoulders, gorilla hands, and a blue-black buccaneer beard; and but for a merry brown eye and a mouth set in perpetual readiness to grin he would have belonged to the "mild-mannered" class, to which, as a matter of fact, he did not. It is written in the lease of his land that he shall drive the Bavicora ranche coach —it's fief-service, it's feudal, and it carries one back. If the little mules and ponies did not stand in the exact six feet of ground where he wanted them, he grabbed hold of them and moved them over to the place without a word, and after being located they never moved until he yanked or lifted them to their place at the pole. The guards were Mexican Indians—hair cut *à la Cosaques*, big straw hats, *serapes*, and munitions of war. William, whose ancestors had emigrated from the Congo region before the war, was

to cook. He was also guide, philosopher, and friend to
Mr. H. and myself in this strange land, and he made all
things possible by his tact and zeal in our behalf. William knows every one in the State of Chihuahua, and he
is constantly telling us of the standing and glittering position of the inhabitants of the mud huts which we pass,
until it sounds like that ghastly array of intelligence with
which a society reporter quickens the social dead in a
Sunday newspaper.

At night we stay at the different ranches, and, rolling
ourselves up in our blankets, we lie down on the mud
floors to sleep. It's not so bad after one becomes used
to it, albeit the skin wears off one's femur joint. The
Mexican hen is as conscientious here as elsewhere, and
we eat eggs. The Mexican coffee is always excellent in
quality, but the people make it up into a nerve-jerking
dose, which will stand hot-water in quantities. Nearly
all travellers are favorably impressed with the *frejoles* and
tortillas of the country. The beans are good, but as old
General Taylor once said, " They killed more men than did
bullets in the Mexican War." Of the *tortillas* I will say, as
my philosophical friend, Mr. Poultney Bigelow, says of the
black bread of the Russian soldier, " It's a good strong food
to march and fight on," which can in no way be a recom-
mendation of its palatability.

The coach starts by gray dawn, and we are aroused at
an early hour. The white men take sponge-baths in a
wash-basin, and the native who stands about deep in the
folds of his *serape* fails utterly to comprehend. He evidently thinks a lot, but he doesn't say anything. I suppose it seems like " clay-eating " or penitent mutilations
to him—not exactly insanity, but a curious custom, at any
rate. On the return trip we have a half-broken team
of buckskin broncos, which have to be " hooked up " with

great stealth. And when the coachman had climbed quietly on to the box and we were inside, the guards let go of the team, and the coachman cracked his whip, while we looked out of the window and held our breath. Then there were Horse Pyrotechniques! Ground and Lofty Tumbling! Greatest Show on Earth! for about a minute, when we made a start down the big road—or didn't, as the case might be. After the first round we often had to get out, and, two ponies having got themselves into the same collar, we would then rearrange them for better luck next time.

In Mexico they drive four mules abreast in the lead and two on the pole, which seems to be an excellent way. Mexican coachmen generally keep "belting" their stock and yelling "*Underlay-nula!*" which is both picturesque and unintelligible. Our man was, however, better educated. Forty or fifty miles is a day's journey, but the exact distance is so dependent on the roads, the load, and the desire to "get thar." that it varies greatly.

We pass the Guerrero stage as it bowls along, and hundreds of heavy, creeking ox-carts, as they draw slowly over the yellow landscape, with their freight to and from the mines. Bunches of sorrowful *burros*, with corn, wood, pottery, and hay, part as we sweep along through and by them.

We have the inspiring vista of Chihuahua before us all the time. It is massive in its proportions and opalescent in color. There are torquois hills, dazzling yellow foregrounds — the palette of the "rainbow school" is everywhere. There are little mud houses, ranches, and dirty little adobe towns to pass, which you must admire, though you may not like them. Gaunt cattle wander in their search for grass and water, and women squat by the riverbed engaged in washing or filling their *ollas*.

The people are enchanting. It is like reading the Bible

to look at them, because it is so unreal; yet there they
are before one, strange and mysterious, and, like other
things which appeal to one's imagination, it would be a
sad thing if one were to understand them. One is tempted
to think that the people of our Northern races know too
much for their own good. It seems remorseless, but it
is so. When I heard the poor Mexican asked why he
thought it had not rained in eighteen months, he said,
" Because God wills it, I suppose;" we were edified by
the way they shifted the responsibility which Farmer
Dunn in our part of the world so cheerfully assumes.

One afternoon we were on a down-grade, going along
at a fair pace, when a wheel struck a stone, placed there
by some freighter to block his load. It heaved the coach,
pulled out the king-pin, and let the big Concord down and
over on its side. The mules went on with the front wheels,
pulling Jack off the box, while we who were on top described a graceful parabolic curve and landed with three
dull thuds. I was caught under the coach by one leg
and held there. A guard inside made all haste to crawl
out through a window, and after a bit I was released.
We were all pretty badly bruised up, and Mr. H. had his
foot broken. The mules were recovered, however, the
coach righted, and we were again off. We made the
town of Tamochica that night, and the town-folks were
kind and attentive. They made crutches, heated water,
and sent a man to the creek to catch leeches to put on
our wounds. Two men were shot in a house near by
during the night, and for a few minutes there was a
lively fusillade of pistol shots. It was evident that life
in Tamochica would spoil a man's taste for anything
quiet, and so as soon as we could move we did it.

We passed an old church, and were shown two Jesuits
who had been dead over a hundred years. They were

HARNESSING MULES

wonderfully preserved, and were dressed in full regalia. I wondered by what embalmer's art it had been accomplished.

A guard of punchers met us to conduct us over a mountain-pass. They were dressed in terra-cotta buckskin trimmed with white leather, and were armed for the largest game in the country. The Bavicora coach has never been robbed, and it is never going to be—or, at least that is the intention of the I-F folks. One man can rob a stage-coach as easily as he could a box of sardines, but with outriders before and behind it takes a large party, and even then they will leave a "hot trail" behind them.

One morning as I was lolling out of the window I noticed the wheel of the coach pass over a long, blue Roman candle. I thought it was curious that a long, blue Roman candle should be lying out there on the plains, when with a sudden sickening it flashed upon me—"giant powder!" The coach was stopped, and we got out. The road was full of the sticks of this high explosive. A man was coming down the road leading a *burro* and picking up the things, and he explained that they had dropped out of a package from his bull-wagon as he passed the night before. We didn't run over any more pieces. If the stick had gone off there would have been a little cloud of dust on the Guerrero road, and, I hope, some regrets in various parts of the world. The incident cannot be made startling, but it put the occupants of the Bavicora coach in a quiet train of reflection that makes a man religious.

Now, as I ponder over the last stage-coach ride which I shall ever take on this earth, I am conscious that it was pleasant, instructive, and full of incident. All that might have happened did not, but enough did to satiate my taste.

STUBBLE AND SLOUGH IN DAKOTA

NOW I am conscious that all my life I have seen men who owned shot-guns and setter-dogs, and that these persons were wont at intervals to disappear from their usual haunts with this paraphernalia. Without thinking, I felt that they went to slay little birds, and for them I entertained a good-natured contempt. It came about in this wise that I acquired familiarity with "mark," and "hie-on," and "No. 6 vis No. 4's": by telegram I was invited to make one of a party in Chicago, bound West on a hunting expedition. It being one of my periods of unrest, I promptly packed up my Winchester, boots, saddle, and blankets, wired "All right—next train," and crawled into the "Limited" at Forty-second Street.

"West" is to me a generic term for that country in the United States which lies beyond the high plains, and this will account for my surprise when I walked into the private car at the St. Paul depot in Chicago and met my friends contesting the rights of occupancy with numerous setter-dogs, while all about were shot-gun cases and boxes labelled "Ammunition." After greetings I stepped to the station platform and mingled with the crowd — disgusted, and disposed to desert.

A genial young soldier who appreciated the curves in my character followed me out, and explained, in the full flush of his joyous anticipation, that we were going to North Dakota to shoot ducks and prairie chicken, and that it would be the jolliest sort of a time; besides, it was a party of good friends. I hesitated, yielded, and enlisted for the enterprise. Feeling now that I was this far it would be good to go on and learn what there was in the form of sport which charmed so many men whose taste I

A DAKOTA CHICKEN-WAGON

respected in other matters, and once embarked I summoned my enthusiasm, and tried to "step high, wide, and handsome," as the horsemen say.

The happiness of a hunting-party is like that of a wedding, so important is it that true love shall rule. The *pièce de résistance* of our car was two old generals, who called each other by an abbreviation of their first names, and interrupted conversations by recalling to each other's memory where some acres of men were slain. "A little more of the roast beef, please—yes, that was where I was shot in this side;" and at night, when quiet reigned and we sought sleep, there would be a waving of the curtains, and a voice, "Oh, say, Blank, do you remember that time my horse was hit with the twelve-pounder?" and it banished dreams. There was a phlebotomist from Pittsburg who had shot all over the earth. He was a thorough sportsman, with a code of rules as complicated as the common-law, and he "made up tough" in his canvas

shooting-clothes. There was a young and distinguished
officer of the regular army who had hunted men, which
excused him in the paltry undertaking before him ; and,
finally, three young men who were adding the accumulated
knowledge of Harvard to their natural endowments.   For
myself, I did not see how jack-boots, spurs, and a Winchester would lend themselves to the stubble and slough
of Dakota, but a collection was taken, and by the time we
arrived in Valley City, Dakota, I was armed, if not ac-

ON THE EDGE OF A SLOUGH

coutred, in the style affected by double-barrel men. All I
now needed was an education, and between the Doctor,
who explained, expostulated, and swore, and a great many
" clean misses," I wore on to the high-school stage. Like

the obliging person who was asked if he played on the violin, I said to myself, " I don't know, but I'll try."

In the early morning three teams drove up where our car was side-tracked, and we embarked in them. The shot-gun man affects buck-colored canvas clothes, with many pockets, and carries his cartridges in his shirt fronts, like a Circassian Cossack. He also takes the shells out of his gun before he climbs into a wagon, or he immediately becomes an object of derision and dread, or, what's worse, suddenly friendless and alone. He also refrains from pointing his gun at any fellow-sportsman, and if he inadvertently does it, he receives a fusillade such as an Irish drill-sergeant throws into a recruit when he does amiss. This day was cool and with a wind blowing, and the poor dogs leaped in delirious joy when let out from their boxes, in which they had travelled all the way from Chicago. After running the wire edge off their nerves they were gotten to range inside a township site, and we jogged along. The first thing which interested me was to hear the Doctor indicate to the driver that he did not care to participate in the driver's knowledge of hunting, and that in order to save mental wear he only had to drive the team, and stand fast when we got out, in order that from the one motionless spot on the prairie sea we could " mark down " the birds.

The immensity of the wheat-fields in Dakota is astonishing to a stranger. They begin on the edge of town, and we drive all day and are never out of them, and on either side they stretch away as far as one's eye can travel. The wheat had been cut and " shocked," which left a stubble some eight inches high. The farm-houses are far apart, and, indeed, not often in sight, but as the threshing was in progress, we saw many groups of men and horses, and the great steam-threshers blowing clouds

A CONFERENCE IN THE MUD

of black smoke, and the flying straw as it was belched from the bowels of the monsters.

During the heat of the day the chickens lie in the cover of the grass at the sides of the fields, or in the rank growth of some slough-hole, but at early morning and evening they feed in the wheat stubble. As we ride along, the dogs range out in front, now leaping gracefully along, now stopping and carrying their noses in the air to detect some scent, and finally—"There's a point! Stop, driver!" and we pile out, breaking our guns and shoving in the cartridges.

"No hurry—no hurry," says the Doctor; "the dog will stay there a month." But, fired with the anticipations, we move briskly up. "You take the right and I'll take the left. Don't fire over the dog," adds the portly sportsman, with an admonishing frown. We go more slowly, and suddenly, with a "whir," up get two chickens and go sailing off. Bang! bang! The Doctor bags his and I miss mine. We load and advance, when up comes the remainder of the covey, and the bewildering plenty of the flying objects rattles me. The Doctor shoots well, and indeed prairie-chickens are not difficult, but I am discouraged. As the great sportsman Mr. Soapy Sponge used to say, "I'm a good shooter, but a bad hitter." It was in this distressful time that I remembered the words of the old hunter who had charge of my early education in .45 calibres, which ran, "Take yer time, sonny, and always see your hind sight," and by dint of doing this I soon improved to a satisfactory extent. The walking over the stubble is good exercise, and it becomes fascinating to watch the well-trained Llewellyn setters "make game," or stand pointing with their tails wagging violently in the nervous thrill of their excitement, then the shooting, and the marking down of the birds who escape the fire, that we may go to them for another "flush." With care and patience one can bag at last the whole covey.

At noon we met the other wagons in a green swale, and had lunch, and, seated in a row under the shadow side of a straw stack, we plucked chickens, while the phlebotomist did the necessary surgery to prepare them for the cook. At three o'clock the soldier, a couple of residents, and myself started together for the evening shooting. We banged away at a thousand-yards range at some teal on a big marsh, but later gave it up, and confined ourselves to chicken. In the midst of a covey and a lot of banging I heard the Captain uttering distressful cries. His gun was leaning on a wheat "shock," and he was clawing himself wildly. "Come, help me—I am being eaten alive." Sure enough he was, for in Dakota there is a little insect which is like a winged ant, and they go in swarms, and their bite is sharp and painful. I attempted his rescue, and

was attacked in turn, so that we ended by a precipitous
retreat, leaving the covey of chickens and their protectors,
the ants, on the field.

We next pushed a covey of grouse into some standing
oats, and were tempted to go in a short way, but some
farmers who were threshing on the neighboring hill blew
the engine whistle and made a "sortie," whereat we
bolted. At a slough which we were tramping through
to kick up some birds "marked down," one suddenly got
up under our feet and flew directly over the Captain, who
yelled "Don't shoot!" as he dropped to the ground. It

"DON'T SHOOT!"

was a well-considered thing to do, since a flying bird looks
bigger than a man to an excited and enthusiastic sportsman. We walked along through the stubble until the red
sunset no longer gave sufficient light, and then got into
our wagon to do the fourteen miles to our car and supper.
Late at night we reached our car, and from it could hear
"the sound of revelry." The cook did big Chicago beef-

steaks by the half-dozen, for an all day's tramp is a sauce which tells.

After some days at this place we were hauled up to Devil's Lake, on the Great Northern road, which locality is without doubt the best for duck-shooting in Dakota. We were driven some sixteen miles to a spur of the lake, where we found a settler. There were hundreds of teal in the water back of his cabin, and as we took position well up the wind and fired, they got up in clouds, and we had five minutes of shooting which was gluttony. We gave the "bag" to the old settler, and the Doctor admonished him to "fry them," which I have no doubt he did.

It was six miles to a pond said to be the best evening shooting about there, and we drove over. There we met our other two teams and another party of sportsmen. The shallow water was long and deeply fringed with rank marsh grass. Having no wading-boots can make no difference to a sportsman whose soul is great, so I floundered in and got comfortably wet. After shooting two or three mud-hens, under the impression that they were ducks, the Doctor came along, and with a pained expression he carefully explained what became of people who did not know a teal from a mud-hen, and said further that he would let it pass this time. As the sun sank, the flight of ducks began, and from the far corners of the marsh I saw puffs of smoke and heard the dull slump of a report.

"Mark—left," came a voice from where the young Harvard man with the peach complexion and the cream hair had ensconced himself in the grass, and, sure enough, a flight was coming towards my lair. I waited until it was nearly over, when I rose up and missed two fine shots, while the Harvard man scored. The birds fell well out in the pond, and he waded out to retrieve them.

As I stood there the soft ooze of the marsh grad-

"MARK—LEFT"

ually swallowed me, and when in answer to the warning
"mark" of my fellows I squatted down in the black water to my middle, and only held my gun and cartridges
up, I began to realize that when a teal-duck is coming
down wind you have got to aim somewhere into the
space ahead of it, hoping to make a connection between
your load of shot and the bird. This I did, and after a
time got my first birds. The air was now full of flying
birds—mallards, spoon-bills, pintails, red-heads, butter-balls,
gadwalls, widgeon, and canvas-backs — and the shooting
was fast and furious. It was a perfect revelry of slaugh-
ter. "Mark—mark." Bang—bang. "What's the matter of that shot?" The sun has set, and no longer bathes
the landscape in its golden light, and yet I sit in the

water and mud and indulge this pleasurable taste for
gore, wondering why it is so ecstatic, or if my companions will not give over shooting presently.   There is little
probability of that, however.   Only darkness can end the
miseries of the poor little teal coming home to their
marsh, and yet with all my sentimental emotions of sympathy I deplore a miss.   If slough-shooting has a draw-
back, it is its lack of action—it is a calm, deliberate shedding of blood, and a wounding of many birds, who die in
the marshes, or become easy prey for the hawks, and it's
as cold-blooded as sitting in water can make it.

We give over at last, and the fortunates change their
wet clothes, while those who have no change sit on the
seat knee-deep in dead birds and shiver while we rattle
homeward.   Our driver gets himself lost, and we bring up

" MARK !"

against a wire fence. Very late at night we struck the
railroad, and counted telegraph poles and travelled east
until the lights of the town twinkled through the gloom.
Once in the car, we find the creature comfort which rec-

TROOPING HOMEWARD IN THE AFTER-GLOW

onciles one to life, and we vote the day a red-letter one.
The goose-shooting came later than our visit, but the
people tell marvellous tales of their numbers. They em-
ploy special guns in their pursuit, which are No. 4 gauge,
single-barrelled, and very long. They throw buckshot
point-blank two hundred yards, and are, indeed, curi-
ous-looking arms. The chicken-shooting is not laborious,
since one rides in a wagon, and a one-lunged, wooden-
legged man is as good as a four-mile athlete at it. He
must know setter-dogs, who are nearly as complicated as

women in their temper and ways; he must have a nose for cover, and he can be taught to shoot; he can keep statistics if he desires, but his first few experiences behind the dogs will not tempt him to do that unless his modesty is highly developed. If he become a shot-gun enthusiast he will discover a most surprising number of fellows—doctors, lawyers, butchers, farmers, and Indians not taxed— all willing to go with him or to be interested in his tales.

The car was to be attached to an express train bound west that night, to my intense satisfaction, and I crawled into the upper berth to dream of bad-lands elk, soldiers, cowboys, and only in the haze of fleeting consciousness could I distinguish a voice—

"Remington, I hope you are not going to fall out of that upper berth again to-night."

POLICING THE YELLOWSTONE

"CAPTAIN ANDERSON — he's the superintendent, you know—started to-day for the south of the Park; some trouble, I believe, down there. A scout thought the buffalo were being disturbed," said Lieutenant Lindsley to me at the Mammoth Hot Springs Hotel, near the entrance to the Park.

"That's unfortunate. Can I overtake him?"

"It's nearly four o'clock, but as I am going down to our camp at the Lower Geyser Basin, we can start now, and by travelling at night we can catch him before he pulls out in the morning, I think," said the yellow-leg.

So putting our belongings into a double surry, we started hot-foot through the Wonderland, leaving a band of Dakota chicken-shooters standing on the steps waving their adieux. It verified all my predictions — men who shoot chickens belong in a stage-coach — they are a "scrubby wagon outfit," as the cowboys say.

Posed on the trestled road, I looked back at the Golden Gate Pass. It is one of those marvellous vistas of mountain scenery utterly beyond the pen or brush of any man. Paint cannot touch it, and words are wasted. War, storms at sea, and mountain scenery are bigger than any expression little man has ever developed. Mr. Thomas Moran made a famous stagger at this pass in his painting; and great as is the painting, when I contemplated the pass itself I marvelled at the courage of the man who dared the deed. But as the stages of the Park Company run over this road, every tourist sees its grandeur, and bangs away with his kodak.

As we pulled up in front of the tents of the rest camp, one of those mountain thunder-storms set in, and it was as though the New York fire department had concentrated its nozzles on the earth. The place was presided over by a classic Irishman by the name of Larry, who speedily got a roaring-hot beefsteak and some coffee on the table, and then busied himself conducting growing pools of rain-water out of the tent. Larry is justly famous on the road for his *bonhomie* and Celtic wit.

At an early hour we arose and departed — the pale moon shining through the mist of the valley, while around us rose the ghostly pines. We cowered under our great-coats, chilled through, and saddened at remembrances of the warm blankets which we had been compelled to roll out of at this unseemly hour. At 7.30 we broke into one of those beautiful natural parks, the Lower Geyser Basin, with the sun shining on the river and the grass, and spotting the row of tents belonging to D Troop, Sixth United States Cavalry. Captain Scott met us at the door, a bluff old trooper in field rig and a welcoming smile. After breakfast a soldier brought up Pat Rooney. Pat was a horse from the ground up; he came from Missouri, but he was a true Irishman nevertheless, as one could tell from his ragged hips, long drooping quarters, and a liberal show of white in his eye, which seemed to say to me, "Aisy, now, and I'm a dray-horse; but spare the brad, or I'll put ye on yer back in the bloomin' dust, I will." The saddle was put on, and I waited, until presently along came the superintendent, with his scout Burgess, three soldiers, and nine pack-mules with their creaking *aparejos*, and their general air of malicious mischief.

Pointing to a range of formidable - looking hills, the

captain said, "We will pull in about there," and we mounted and trotted off down the road. What a man really needs when he does the back stretches of the Yellowstone Park is a boat and a balloon, but cavalrymen ride horses in deference to traditions. My mount, Pat, was as big as a stable door, and as light as a puff-ball on his pins. As Mr. Buckram said, "The 'eight of a 'oss 'as nothing to do with 'is size," but Patrick was a horse a man needed two legs for. Besides, he had a mouth like a bull, as does every other animal that wears that impossible bit which Uncle Sam gives his cavalry. We got along swimmingly, and, indeed, I feel considerable gratitude to Pat for the two or three thousand times he saved my life on the trip by his agility and sureness of foot.

BURGESS, NEARLY FORTY-FIVE YEARS A SCOUT

Burgess, the scout, was a fine little piece of a man, who
had served the government with credit for over thirty
years. He had breasted the high divide in a dozen places,
had Apache bullets whistle around and through him, and
withal was modest about it. He was a quiet person, with
his instinct of locality as well developed as an Indian's,
and contented with life, since he only wanted one thing—
a war. I think he travelled by scent, since it would have
been simple enough to have gone over easier places; but
Burgess despised ease, and where the fallen timber was
thickest and the slopes 60°, there you would find Burgess
and his tight little pony picking along.

Both Captains Anderson and Scott have a pronounced
weakness for geysers, and were always stopping at every
little steam-jet to examine it. I suppose they feel a personal responsibility in having them go regularly; one can
almost imagine a telegram to "turn on more steam."
They rode recklessly over the geyser formation, to my
discomfort, because it is very thin and hazardous, and to
break through is to be boiled. One instinctively objects
to that form of cooking. The most gorgeous colors are
observed in this geyser formation; in fact, I have never
seen nature so generous in this respect elsewhere. I wondered that the pack-mules did not walk into the sissing
holes, but I suspect a mule is a bit of a geologist in his
way, and as most of them have been in the government
service for thirty or forty years, they have learned how to
conserve their well-being. There is a tradition that one
was considerably overdone once in a geyser-hole, so they
may have taken warning. Who can understand a mule?
The packer leads the old bell-mare off to a feeding-
ground, and the whole bunch of mules go racing after
her, and chains wouldn't hold them. The old bell-mare
takes across a nasty chasm or a dirty slough-hole, and as

THE BELL-MARE OVER A BAD PLACE

the tinkle of the little cow-bell is losing itself in the timber beyond, one after another they put their ears forward
and follow on.

We passed up a cleft in the hills, and were swallowed
up in the pine and cedar forest. Presently the cleft
ended, and nothing but good honest climbing was in
front. There began my first experience in riding over
the fallen timber, which obstructs all the northwestern
Rocky Mountains. Once up in British Columbia I did
it, but had trails, and I childishly imagined that there
must also be trails wherever men wanted to go. Criss-
cross and all about lay the great peeled logs, and travel

was slow, toilsome, and with anything but horses trained
to it would have been impossible.

A good horse or mule, once accustomed, makes little
of it, but on the steep down grades the situation is complicated by fallen logs, which it is necessary to " bucket "
over, and then stop dead on an incline of 50°, with a
couple of miles of tumble if he fails. The timber grew
thicker, and when Burgess would get us in a hopeless
sort of place, Captain A. would sing out to Captain S.,
" Burgess is on the trail now "; and when it was fairly
good going, " Now he is off." But nothing could rattle
Mr. Burgess, and he continued calmly on his journey, the
destination of which, it seemed, could be nothing short of
the moon. Finally we found ourselves seemingly so in-
extricably tangled up that even Burgess had to scratch
his head. One mule was hung up hopelessly, while the
rest crowded around us into the *chevaux-de-frise* of logs,
and merrily wound through the labyrinth the old Sixth
Cavalry " gag," " Here's where we trot."

To complete the effect of this passage it began to rain,
and shortly to pelt us with hailstones, so we stopped
under some trees to let it pass, and two people who
should know better dismounted and got their saddles
wet, while another, more wise in his generation, sat tight,
and was rewarded later for his display of intelligence.
By-and-by, wet and tired of fallen timber, we came into
the Little Fire-hole Basin, and found buffalo signs in
abundance. We were in great hopes of seeing some of
these animals, but I may as well add that only one was
seen on the trip, though there was fresh spoor, and they
were undoubtedly about. We found no pony tracks
either, which was more to the soldiers' liking, since they
are intrusted with the protection of the Park against
poachers.

DOWN THE MOUNTAIN

In this way squads are sent over the Park, and instruct-
ed not to follow the regular trails, but to go to the most
unfrequented places, so that they may at any time happen on a malicious person, and perhaps be able to do as
one scout did—photograph the miscreant with his own
camera.

After a good day's march we made camp by a little
lake, and picketed our horses, while the mules ran loose
around the bell-mare. Our appetites had been sharp-
ened by a nine hours' fast, when a soldier called us to the
" commissaries " which were spread out on a pack canvas.
It was the usual military " grub," and no hungry man can
find fault with that.

" Any man who can't eat bacon can't fight," as Captain
Scott said ; so if any reader wants to be a soldier he must
have a mania for bacon, it seems.   " This is the stuff that
makes soldiers brave," he added, as the coffee-pot came
around, and we fell to, and left a dreary waste of empty
tins for the cook to pick up. We lighted our pipes after
the banquet on the grass, and walked down to the shore
of the beautiful pond, which seemed so strangely situated
up there on the very crest of the continental divide.
There are only three seasons in these altitudes, which the
boys divide into July, August, and Winter, and the nights
are always chilly. An inch or two of snow may fall even
in mid-summer. In winter the snow covers the ground
to a great depth, as we can tell by the trees. Nothing
grows but rather stunted fir and pine and a little grass of
the most hardy variety. The rounds of the Park are then
made by mounting the cavalry on the *ski*, or Norwegian
snow-shoe, and with its aid men travel the desolate snow-
clad wilderness from one " shack " to another. Small
squads of three or four men are quartered in these remote recesses of the savage mountains, and remain for

eight months on a stretch. The camps are provisioned for the arctic siege, and what is stranger yet is that soldiers rather like it, and freely apply for this detached service. There is little of the "pomp and vanity" in this soldiering, and it shows good spirit on the part of the enlisted men. They are dressed in fur caps, California blanket coats, leggings, and moccasins — a strange uniform for a cavalryman, and also quite a commentary on what are commonly called the vicissitudes of the service.

In the early morning our tent was pulled down, and our bedding packed off almost before we had disentan-

GETTING GRUB

gled ourselves from its sheltering folds. The well-trained troopers went about their task of breaking camp with method and address. Burgess and a young soldier pulled a reluctant strawberry-blond mule out of the line of pack-animals, and throwing a blind over his face, proceeded to lay the blanket and adjust the *aparejo*. With a heave the *cincha* is hauled tight, and the load laid on, while the expert throws the " diamond hitch," and the mule and pack are integral parts. This packing of nine mules was accomplished with great rapidity, and laying our saddles carefully, we mounted and followed the scouts off down the trail in single file on a toilsome march which would probably not end until three or four o'clock in the afternoon. We wound around the spurs of hills, and then across a marsh, with its yielding treacherous bottom, where the horses floundered, and one mule went down and made the mud and water fly in his struggles, while my apprehensions rose to fever-pitch as I recognized my grip-sack on his load, and not likely to be benefited by the operation. At the head-waters of these rivers—and it may be said that this little purling brook is really the source of the Missouri itself, although not so described— there is abundance of soggy marsh, which makes travel extremely difficult. In one place Captain Anderson's horse went belly-deep on a concealed quag made by a stream coming out of the side of the hill, and rolling back, fell heavily on the captain, and for a time it was rather a question whether the horse would get out or not ; but by dint of exertion he regained firm ground. When a big strong horse gets into a slough the dorsal action is terrific, and it is often necessary to dismount quickly to aid him out. We crossed the great divide of the continent at a place where the slope was astonishingly steep and the fallen timber thickly strewn. It was

WORKING UP THE DIVIDE

BURGESS FINDING A FORD

as thoroughly experimental travelling as I have ever seen, unless possibly over a lava-rock formation which I essayed last winter on the western slope of the Sierra Madre, in Chihuahua ; and yet there is a fascination about being balanced on those balloonlike heights, where a misstep means the end of horse and rider. I was glad enough, though, when we struck the parklike levels of the Pitch-stone plateau as the scene of our further progression. If one has never travelled horseback over the Rocky Mountains there is a new and distinct sensation before him quite as vigorous as his first six-barred gate, or his first yacht-race with the quarter-rail awash.

All through the Park were seen hundreds of wild-geese, so tame that they would hardly fly from us. It was a great temptation to shoot, but the doughty captain said he would run me off the reservation at a turkey-trot if I did shoot, and since I believed him I could restrain myself. The streams and marshes were full of beaver-dams, and the little mud-and-stick houses rose from the pools, while here and there we saw the purl of the quiet water as they glided about. This part is exactly as primitive as when the lonely trapper Coulter made his famous journey through it, and one cannot but wonder what must have been his astonishment at the unnatural steaming and boiling of the geysers, which made the Park known from his descriptions as "Coulter's Hell."

From the breast of the mountains overlooking the great Shoshonee Lake there opened up the most tremendous sight as the waters stretched away in their blue placidity to the timbered hills. The way down to the shores was the steepest place I have ever seen horses and mules attempt. In one place, where the two steep sides of the cañon dipped together, it was cut by a nasty seam some six feet deep, which we had to "bucket over" and maintain a footing on the other side. After finding myself safely over, I watched the shower of pack-mules come sliding down and take the jump. One mule was so far overbalanced that for a moment I thought he would lose his centre of gravity, which had been in his front feet, but he sprang across to the opposite slope and was safe. Horses trained to this work do marvels, and old Pat was a "topper" at the business. I gave him his head, and he justified my trust by negotiating all the details without a miss. On a sandy "siding" he spread his feet and slid with an avalanche of detached hill-side. Old Pat's ears stuck out in front in an anxious way, as if to say, "If we hit anything solid, I'll stop"; while from behind came the cheery voice of Captain Scott, "Here's where we trot."

On the shores of the Shoshonee we camped, and walked over to the famous Union Geysers, which began to boil and sputter, apparently for our especial benefit. In a few minutes two jets of boiling water shot a hundred feet in air, and came down in rain on the other side, while a rainbow formed across it. The roar of the great geysers was awe-inspiring; it was like the exhaust of a thousand locomotives, and Mr. Burgess nudged me and remarked, " Hell's right under here."

Near the geysers, hidden away in a depression, we found a pool of water of a beautiful and curious green, while not twenty feet from it was one of a sulphur yellow. There was a big elk track in the soft mud leading into it, but no counter track coming out. There had been a woodland tragedy there.

The utility of a geyser-hole is not its least attraction to a traveller who has a day's accumulation of dust and sweat on him. I found one near the camp which ran into a little mountain stream, and made a tepid bath, of which I availed myself, and also got a cup of hot water, by the aid of which I "policed my face," as the soldiers call shaving.

The next day we encountered one of those great spongy mountain meadows, which we were forced to skirt on the rocky timber-strewn hill-sides, until finally we ventured into it. We curved and zigzagged through its treacherous mazes, fording and recrossing the stream in search of solid ground. Burgess's little gray pony put his foot forward in a gingerly way, and when satisfied, plunged in and floundered through. The pony had a positive genius for morasses. We followed him into the mud, or plunged off the steep sides into the roaring river, and, to my intense satisfaction, at last struck a good pony trail. "Now Burgess is off the trail!" we cried, whereat the modest little scout grinned cheerfully. From here on it was "fair and easy," until we came to the regular stage-road, to travel on which it seemed to us a luxury.

This expedition is typical of the manner of policing the Park, and it is generally monotonous, toilsome, and uneventful work; and the usefulness of such a *chevauchée* is that it leaves the track of the cavalry horse-shoe in the most remote parts of the preserve, where the poacher or interloper can see it, and become apprehensive in consequence of the dangers which attend his operations. That an old trapper might work quietly there for a long time I do not doubt, if he only visited his line of traps in the early morning or late evening and was careful of his trail, but such damage as he could do would be trivial. Two regiments could not entirely prevent poaching in the mountain wastes of the great reservation, but two troops are successful enough at the task. It is a great game-preserve and breeding-ground, and, if not disturbed, must always give an overflow into

Montana, Wyoming, and Idaho, which will make big game shooting there for years to come. The unreasoning antipathy or malicious disregard of the American pioneer for game-laws and game-preservation is somewhat excusable, but the lines of the pioneer are now cast in new places, and his days of lawless *abandon* are done. The regulation for the punishment of Park offenders is inadequate, and should be made more severe. The Park is also full of beasts of prey, the bear being very numerous. A fine grizzly was trapped by some of the superintendent's men and shipped to the Smithsonian Institution while I was there. Near the Fountain Hotel one evening a young army surgeon and myself walked up to within one hundred and fifty yards of a big grizzly, who was not disposed to run off. Being unarmed, we concluded that our point of view was close enough, and as the bear seemed to feel the same way about it, we parted.

Americans have a national treasure in the Yellowstone Park, and they should guard it jealously. Nature has made her wildest patterns here, has brought the boiling waters from her greatest depths to the peaks which bear eternal snow, and set her masterpiece with pools like jewels. Let us respect her moods, and let the beasts she nurtures in her bosom live, and when the man from Oshkosh writes his name with a blue pencil on her sacred face, let him spend six months where the scenery is circumscribed and entirely artificial.

A MODEL SQUADRON

I AM not quite sure that I should not say "The Model Colonel," since every one knows men and horses are much alike when they have first passed under the eye of the recruiting officer and the remount board, and every one knows that colonels are very unlike, so that a model squadron or a model troop is certain to owe its superiority to its commander; but as we are observing the product in this instance, let the title stand as above stated.

The model squadron aforesaid is quartered across the Potomac from Washington in Fort Meyer, which is the only purely·cavalry post in the country. Everywhere else the troops are mixed, and the commandant may be of any arm of the service. Here they are all cavalry, with cavalry officers and cavalry ideas, and are not hindered by dismounted theories, or pick-and-shovel work, or any of the hundreds of things which hamper equally good "yellow legs" in other posts. There are many passable misdemeanors in this post, but only one crime, and that is bad riding. There is little dismounted work, and any soldier can have his horse out on a pass, so long as he does not abuse the privilege; and when he does, it's plenty of walking falls to his lot.

There is a large brick riding-hall of approved pattern, which enables the men to do their work in all weathers. The four troops now quartered there are from the First, Seventh, Eighth, and Ninth regiments, which creates a good - natured rivalry, very conducive to thorough work. It is the opinion of General Henry that one old troop should always be left at this post as a pace-setter for the newly transferred ones, which seems reasonable.

Now to tell what the preparatory discipline is to the magnificent riding which can be seen any morning by spectators who are " game for a journey " to the fort by ten o'clock, I must say that General Guy V. Henry is a flaming fire of cavalry enthusiasm.   He has one idea—a

GENERAL GUY V. HENRY, SEVENTH UNITED STATES CAVALRY

great broad expanse of principle—ever so simple in itself, but it is basic, and nothing can become so complicated that he cannot revert to his simple idea and by it regulate the whole. It is the individual training of the horse and rider. One bad rider or one unbroken horse can disarrange the whole troop movement, and "woe to him" who is not up to concert pitch! "Who is the scoundrel, the lummux, humph?" and the colonel, who is a brevet-brigadier-general, strides up and down, and fire comes from his nostrils. "Prefer charges against him, captain!" and the worst befalls. The unfortunate trooper has committed the highest crime which the commandant of Fort Meyer knows—he cannot ride.

A soldier becomes a rider by being bucketed about on a bareback horse, or he dies. The process is simple, the tanbark soft, and none have died up to date, but all have attained the other alternative. This is unimportant; but the horse — it is to his education that the oceans of patience and the mountains of intelligence are brought to bear. It is all in the books if any one cares to go into it. It is the gathering of the horse; it is the legs carried to the rear of the girths; it is the perfect hand and the instant compliance of the horse with the signs as indicated by the rider; it is the backing, the passaging, the leading with either foot, and the pivoting on the front legs; it is the throwing of horses, the acquisition of gaits, and the nice bitting; it is one hundred little struggles with the brute until he comes to understand and to know that he must do his duty. It all looks beautifully simple, but in practice we know that while it is not difficult to teach a horse, it is quite another matter to unteach him, so in these horses at least no mistakes have been made. After all this, one fine sunny Friday morning the people drove out from Washington in their traps and filed into

RIDING SITTING ON LEGS

the galleries and sat down—fair women and brave men;
of the former we are sure, and of the latter we trust. The
colonel blew a whistle—ye gods, what a sacrilege against
all the traditions of this dear old United States army!—
and in rode Captain Bomus's troop of the First Plungers,
which I cannot but love, since I am an honorary member
of their officers' mess, and fondly remember the fellows
who are now sniffing alkali dust down in Arizona. They
were riding with blankets and surcingles, and did their
part of a drill, the sequence of which I have forgotten,
since it was divided with the three other troops—Captain
Bell's, of the Seventh, Captain Hughes's, of the Ninth,
and Captain Fountain's, of the Eighth. I felt a strong

personal interest in some of these men, for memory took
me back to a night's ride in Dakota with a patrol of the
Ninth, when they were all wrapped in buffalo-skin overcoats, with white frost on their lapels; the horses' noses
wore icicles, and the dry snow creaked under the tread of
the hoofs as we rode over the starlit plain and through the
black shadows of the *coulees*. I had pounded along also
through the dust in the wake of this troop of the Eighth
when it wasn't so cold, but was equally uncomfortable.

OVER THE HURDLE BACK TO BACK

The sharp commands of the captain soon put the troop
in motion, and they trotted along with a cadenced tread,
every man a part of his horse; they broke into fours and
wheeled to the right about, then into line and wound

themselves up in the "spiral," and unwound again, and soon brought order out of a mess, and the regular canter was ever the same. Then low hurdles were strung across the hall, and by column of fours the troop went over, never breaking the formation ; to the rear they turned and back again ; finally they took the obstacle in line, and every horse rose as though impelled by the same mechanism. As if this was not enough, every second man was dismounted and put on double with a comrade, not with his breast to his comrade's back, but back to back, and then in line the odd cavalcade charged the hurdles, and took them every one. It was not an individual bucketing of one horse after another, but all in line and all together. After this what could there be more to test the "glue" in these troopers' seats? There was more, however, and in this wise : The saddles were put on, but without any girths, and all the movements were gone through with again, ending up with a charge down the hall, and bringing up against the wall of the spectators' stand at a sharp "halt," which would have unseated a monkey from a trick-mule.

The horses were all thrown by pulling their heads about, and one cavalryman amused himself by jumping over his prostrate mount. They rode " at will," and stood upon their knees on their horses' backs. One big animal resented carrying double, and did something which in Texas would be called "pitching," but it was scarcely a genuine sample, since the grinning soldiers made little of it.

The troop of the Ninth executed a "left backward turn" with beautiful precision, and this difficult undertaking will serve to give one an idea of the training of the mounts.

Gymnastics of all sorts were indulged in, even to the

THROWING A HORSE

extent of turning summersaults over four horses from a
spring-board.   A citizen near me, whose mind had probably wandered back to Barnum and Bailey, said:

"But what's this got to do with soldiers; is it not
highly flavored with circus?"

I could offer no excuse except the tradition that cavalrymen are supposed to ride well.   All the men were
young and in first-rate physical fix, and seemed to enjoy

the thing—all except one old first sergeant, who had been time - expired these half - dozen times, whose skin was so full of bullet-holes that it wouldn't hold blood, and who had entered this new régime with many protests :

"O'me nau circus ape; I can't be leppin' around afther the likes av thim!" whereat the powers arranged it so that the old veteran got a job looking after plug tobacco, tomato-cans, tinned beef, and other "commissaries," upon which he viewed the situation more cheerfully.

The drill was tremendously entertaining to the ladies and gentlemen in the gallery, and they clapped their hands and went bustling into their traps and off down the road to the general's house, where Madam the General gave a breakfast, and the women no doubt asked the second lieutenants deliciously foolish questions about their art. The gentlemen, some of whom are Congressmen and other exalted governmental functionaries, felt proud of the cavalry, and went home with a determination to combat any one hostile to cavalry legislation, if a bold front and firm purpose could stay the desecrating hand.

But all this work is primary and elementary. The second degree is administered in field-work, comprising experimental marches, and those who know General Henry by reputation will not forget his hundred-mile march with the Ninth Cavalry at Pine Ridge, and those who know him personally will become acquainted with his theory that a cavalry command in good condition, with proper feeds, should make fifty miles a day, with a maximum on the road of ten hours a day, moving at the rate of five miles an hour in cavalry halts, the gaits being walk, trot, and leading, with a day's rest each week, to be continued indefinitely. And knowing all this, they will be sure that the model squadron wears out a good many horseshoes in a season.

The " Cossack outposts " are another feature much insisted on, and, strange to say, this arrangement was first invented in America, despite its name (see Wagner's *Outposts*), and is an improvement on picket posts in a ratio of 240 to 324. Another movement is the " form square," which is an adaptation of the " Indian circle," it being a movement from a centre to a circle, and useful when escorting wagons or when surprised. The non-commissioned officers are sent on reconnoissance, on patrols, and are required to make maps, which are submitted to an inspector.

Another scheme which I have never seen was the linking of a troop of horses, formed in a circle, to one another, by hooking the regular cavalry links from one horse's bridle to the next one's halter ring, and then leaving them in charge of one man. I also saw the new cavalry bit for the first time. It is commended by all who use it, and I saw no horses boring on it or in the least uppish about going against it, and I never remember a horse who would not do either the one or the other to the old trap which was formerly worn.

Two other curious movements indulged in by this squadron are the firing over horses while they are lying down; and, riding double — the man faced to the rear draws his pistol, and while moving to the rear keeps shooting. It might be useful during a slow retreat, and could be done with the carbine equally well.

This whole enterprise at Fort Meyer is vastly encouraging. As one officer said, " We take no credit for it, since others could do the same if they had riding-halls and cavalry officers in command." But there are cavalry officers and there are cavalry officers, and it is not every day one is born. For thirty-five years has the old general sat in a McClellan saddle, and the tremendous enthusiasm of newly joined "sub" still remains. The very thought of a wagon arouses his indignation, and every day the mules are brought into the riding-hall, and the men initiated into the intricacies of the "diamond hitch." It takes a past-master to pack a mule in twenty-two seconds, however, and I saw that feat accomplished in General Henry's command.

It is a grand thing for the young men to have this practical training by these old veterans of the civil war and the alkali plains before they go on the retired list. It is well for a young man to know enough not to unsaddle a sweating troop of horses in a broiling sun, and to learn that it makes sore backs; and it is quite important if men can cook rations, and not go up to the sky-line of a hill when scouting, and rival the statue of "Liberty Enlightening the World," when it is clearly their business to throw what light they have behind them and not before. It takes experience to put the sole of a boot back on the upper, when it has fetched loose, with four horseshoe nails, and it is not every man that knows that the place to intrench is on the edge of a cut bank, near water, if one expects ever to get out of a round-up. No one can figure that a recruit will know how many people passed over the road before him, or which way they were going, and it takes a long head and good nerves not to pull a trigger unless the sight is dark on the object when the fight may last all day and probably all night; but all these things are not taught in school. If a horse under him is weakening on a long march in an enemy's country, it is an ignorant fool who uses a spur instead of good sense. That's the time to unload a few dollars' worth of government property. But who can understand the value of a rubber blanket, fifty rounds of ammunition, and a pocket full of grub, with a feed of grain in the bag, but one who

OVER THE HURDLES IN LINE

has tried it? There are lots of dead soldiers who would have learned these lessons if they had been older. In my opinion, the tremendous box of tricks which Uncle Sam's horses are supposed to carry has put more men afoot than will ever be admitted; but at least the old boot has gone, though there is yet room for an intelligent hand with a jack-plane to shave off that cavalry pack. I am inclined to take what every one tells me is a "cranky" view on this subject, but let it stand until the next hard campaign, and I hope to be able to be more lucid. Horses are horses, and horses are not made of wood, iron, or by rule of thumb.

To revert to Fort Meyer: it is altogether refreshing; it is worth any one's while to go there and see four troops of cavalry which cannot be beaten, and it is positively exhilarating to meet their creator, a thoroughly typical United States cavalry officer, and I'm bound to say his successor in command has had a hard pace set for him.

THE AFFAIR OF THE —TH OF JULY

to a street. They were loaded, and then down on the next corner came the order through the still night to fire. A terrific flash illuminated the black square, and then with a howl down the long street went the 2¾-inch, and far down in the darkness I could see her explode; then all was silent. The signal-rockets were going from the top of the Auditorium, and I saw the answering upward sweep of the balls of fire as they were replied to farther down the street. We were on the extreme right, which was below the Art Building, and were ordered to move for an attack on the streets of the city *en échelon*. The guns limbered up, and, escorted by two companies of infantry, we passed into the dim light. At the corner of Wabash Avenue we halted.

Four or five blocks down we could both hear and see rifle-firing, evidently directed on our camp, and also a great crowd. At this juncture we heard a most awful explosion, dull and not like a rifle-canon. " Dynamite !" we all exclaimed in a breath.

" Cut the fuse to zero ! Fire !" And with a terrific crash the missile sped on its way. " I think that street will be clear for a spell," drawled the captain, in his delicious old Georgia manner, as he got his guns in motion. We could hear the occassional boom of a 3-inch and the loud grinding of the Gatlings, and we knew it was enfilading our fire. The rifle-fire was silenced down the city, and the mob, as we judged by the noise, was running away. Over in the direction of the post-office we then heard rifle-shots.

" That's that outpost of the Twenty-seventh guarding the building," we said to each other. It fairly crackled now—" giving 'em hot stuff."

" Halt !" came the command, and the men stopped. " We will wait here for orders."

"What do you suppose that report was?" we asked each other as we stood on the curbing.

"It must have been dynamite. I know the sound of this ordnance too well to be mistaken," commented the captain of artillery. "What's that? Hark!" as a clatter sounded on the pavement in our rear. "It's a horse coming at full speed. Spread out, men, and stop him." And, sure enough, a frightened cavalry horse came charging into the midst of the infantry, and was only stopped after he had knocked down two men.

"He only has a halter on; he's got away from the picket line; here, boys—here comes another." This one in turn was stopped, and two more which followed directly. Detailed men were sent back with the horses, while I went also to make my report. As I sped on ahead I was startled by a shot, and with a sputter I heard the bullet go to pieces at my feet. I looked around, and from the dark of a window came a flash and another sputter.

"D—— him, he is firing at me," I ejaculated, and I made the pedals fly. I had no idea of stopping, but I thought I could remember the building; and thinks I, "I am not after game, but whoever you are, I'll hunt you up, my lad."

At headquarters everything was bustle.

"Some one exploded a big dynamite bomb right in the street, in front of the Fifth Infantry camp," said Captain Moss to me, "and killed four men and wounded a dozen more. Some of the cavalry horses broke away from the picket lines and stampeded," he went on.

The hospital tents were ablaze with light, and I knew that the surgeons were at their grewsome work.

I reported for orders, and shortly was given one to deliver at my old post. Back I sped, and came near tumbling into a big hole, which I knew had been made by the dynamite bomb. I will go down another street and cross over, so as to avoid that fellow who potted at me, I reasoned; but before I turned off I saw the two infantrymen and the four old cavalry horses coming along.

"Oh, lieutenant," they called, and I went up to them. "We saw that fellow shoot at you, and McPherson held the horses and I slipped down the dark side of the street and located him. He stuck his head out of the window, and I rested across a door-post and let him have it."

"Did you hit him?"

"Well, you kin bet! He came out of that window like a turkey out of a pine-tree. A little slow at first, but ker-flop at last."

So I took the street of my late enemy, and had a look at a dark object which lay on the sidewalk under the house I had located. In response to the order I bore, the infantry advanced to develop any opposition which there might be. Men were thrown out in front, and the heavy body marched in rear. We had proceeded this way for some blocks with no sound but the dropping rifle-fire some quarter of a mile to our left and behind us, when we began to find men huddled in doorways, who were promptly taken prisoners and disarmed, and sent to the rear. Some bore rifles and all had revolvers, and a hard-looking set they were. The artillery fire had demoralized them, and whatever they were to have done they had abandoned after the first shell had gone shrieking and crashing down the street.

"They'll get a drum-head in the morning, and it won't sit ten minutes," mused an officer. "I suppose they are anarchists. Well, they ought to like this; this is a sort of anarchy. It's the best we have got in our shop."

These words were scarcely spoken before a blinding flash lit up the street as lightning might. A tremendous report followed, and I was knocked down right over my bicyle, which I was trundling. I was up in an instant, and with a ringing clash an object had fallen at my feet and struck my leg a smart blow, which pained me considerably. I reached down and picked up a Springfield rifle barrel without lock or stock. A dynamite cartridge had been exploded in our front. The infantry hesitated for a moment. Many men had been flung on their backs by the force of the concussion. "Forward!" was the command, and dropping my bicycle, I followed the dark figures of the infantry as they made their way down the sides of the streets. Half a block ahead was a great hole in the pavement, and the sidewalk was littered with cobble-stones and débris from the walls of the surrounding buildings. The bomb had been exploded over the advance-guard, and had destroyed it utterly. Which building had it come from? We stood in the doorways, and held our breath and waited. A stone dropped in the street with a crash. A tiny light appeared in one of the upper windows of a tall narrow office building. It disappeared instantly, and all was dark. Two men put their heads out of the window. "See-e!" I hissed, as a soldier drew up his rifle. All was quiet. The two heads peered down the street, and then whispered together, when shortly we caught the hollow echo of the words, "D—— 'em, they don't want any more."

"Now run for it," said the captain in command, who was a big fellow, and we all scampered off down the street to our main body. What we had discovered was reported to the battery commander. He swore a great oath.

"Bring that gun up here to this side; boost her on to the sidewalk. Come, get hold here, you fellows; lend us a hand ; run her along a little ; train her on that doorway. Now fire !" And then, in a high voice, " Captain, let your men cover that house with rifle-fire, and detail some men to break into a store and get inflammables."

The big gun went with a deafening crash, and the doorway was in slivers. A dropping rifle-fire rained into the windows. Crash went the big gun after a minute, but the building was dark and silent, as though holding their sputtering toys in contempt.

" I'm going to burn that building. Send a man to call out the fire department !" roared the old captain, who had now lost all his drawling, and was bellowing like a bull. After a time infantrymen came along with their arms full of bottles and cans of kerosene, and I know not what else. They had broken into a drug-store, and told the proprietor, who was found there in the darkness with his three clerks, to give them the most inflammable substances at his command.

The squad of infantry formed on the side of the street occupied by the ill-fated house, and as the big gun crashed and the rifle-fire redoubled, they dashed down the street and swarmed into the building.

" Keep up that rifle-fire !" howled the senior officer. It was bang ! bang ! bang ! for a full minute, when a flash of light lit up the doorway, and with a rush out came the squad, and made its way to us on the run.

" We have fired the elevator shaft," said a young officer, breathing heavily with excitement. The doorway was very light now, and shortly the second-story windows over it showed yellow. Windows farther up the tall building began to redden and then to glow brightly. It was ten minutes now since the first gleam of fire, and the rifles had ceased. The building was now ablaze. A huge roaring was heard, and the black smoke poured from the hall windows, while the side windows were yet dark. A harsh yelling came from the window where I had seen the little match struck, and the thick black smoke eddied around and hid it all.

" By sections—forward—trot—march," and with a dash we moved forward past the roaring furnace and down into the darkness below.

"My orders were to move forward," muttered the old captain, as he bit at a plug of tobacco.

It was now nearly twelve o'clock, and I could hear a great deal of small-arm firing down the city on my left in front, and also the boom of cannon away on the other side of town. Shortly a note was handed me by an adjutant, and I was to go to a command on a street nearly in front of headquarters. I sped along, and shortly met men by twos and threes, wounded men going to camp, and two fellows sitting on the curbing. " Where is Captain B——'s command, my men ?"

" Right on down the street—me bunkie's got it," was all I heard as I shot along.

The rifle-fire grew, and the crash of a Hotchkiss came at intervals. Then I made out a small infantry reserve, and then the guns. I found the captain, and delivered my note.

" Wait by me," said the captain, as he went into a doorway and read the order by scratching matches on his pantaloons, and the Hotchkiss nearly broke my ear-drums. " Wait a minute or so," said the captain, as he crushed the note into his trousers-pocket.

I waited, and a " kid " of the reserves, whom I knew, greeted me and explained. " They are in the depot, and we are going to carry it by storm in a minute."

Again the Hotchkiss went, and " Come on !" rang the order as the men moved forward. It was the captain,

and he wanted me to " wait a minute," so, thinks I, I will
wait near him; and pulling my bicycle into a dark doorway, I waited along by the captain, near the head of the
procession. As we moved out from the protection of the
street the report of a Hotchkiss nearly threw me from my
pins, and then we ran silently under a rather hot fire from
the windows and doorways. I heard the balls strike—a
dull slap—and a man stumbled forward ahead of me and
dropped. I sprang over him, and was soon out of fire,
and with the little column passed through the big doorway under which I had so often passed with my gripsack
and on the *qui vive* for a hansom-cab driver. There was a
tremendous rattle of fire, the bullets struck the stone-
work viciously; the hollow pat sounded, and men sank
reeling and lay prone under my feet. We piled in and
returned the fire. It was all smoke now; nothing dis-
tinguishable. " Come on !" came a voice which inter-
larded itself with the reports, and we went on wildly.
We were now out of the smoke, and then I saw, by the
light of a fire, figures running. A man fired in our faces.
He was sitting up ; a bayonet went into him, and he rolled
over, clutching his breast with his hands. " The house is
on fire !" came the cry, and the infantry continued to
discharge on the retreating figures. A great flash lighted
everything, and as my senses returned, it came over me
" that was a bomb." I passed my hand over my eyes.
The building was on fire. I could see men lying around
me breathing heavily and groaning. I got up ; a voice
said, " Get these men out of here !" " Get these men out
of here !" I echoed, as I grabbed a big Irish sergeant, and
supporting him under the arms, I strove forward. The
living soldiers took hold of the dead and wounded comrades, and bore them back through the smoke and into
the street. The station was now on fire, and every one

was highly excited, for these bombs made strange work, and were very demoralizing. They did no particular good to the enemy beyond that point, since they did not stop our advance, and they also demoralized the enemy quite as much as ourselves. There seemed to be no further opposition to the troops. I went back to headquarters, got my horse, and received permission to go with a detachment of cavalry. We pulled out up Michigan Avenue. We were to scout and make a junction with stock-yard troops out to the south of the city or in Washington Park. The moon was going down, and there was no sound but the clattering of the troops and the jingle of the sabres. We passed a large squad of police, with their lanterns, moving out south to protect private residences and arrest prowlers. Ahead of us we heard three revolver-shots, and galloping forward, we were hailed by a voice from a window. "They have been trying to break into my house, catch them ; they are running up the street." The road here was very wide, with two rows of trees in the centre and narrow grass-plots.

"Come on !" shouted the captain, and spurring up, we moved forward.

"There they are, captain : can't you see them ?" spoke the old first sergeant, as he drove his horse forward to the captain's side.

We rode over the grass-plot, and, sure enough, forms were seen to run up the steps of houses and behind shrubbery.

"Dismount !—shoot them down !" came the command, and the men sprang forward with a rush. A revolver flashed, and was followed by a dozen carbine-balls, and from the blackness of a high front stoop rolled a figure grunting and gasping. Shot after shot rang through the darkness, and the troopers routed the vermin from step and shrubbery, until shortly it ceased.

"WE WERE NOW OUT OF THE SMOKE"

"Captain, here is Foltz—he's been shot; and McIner-ny—he's shot too."

I sprang up the steps of a great stone mansion and pounded on the door with the butt of my six-shooter. A window was raised and a head peered out. "What do you want?"

"We are United States cavalry, and we have two wounded men. Open your doors; we want you to put them to bed," and the window went down with a bang. Shortly the bolts were drawn, the door opened, and an old gentleman with white hair and carrying a lamp appeared.

"Certainly; bring them right in, captain," said the old gentleman, and the two men were carefully lifted and borne in by their comrades. I helped to carry one man up-stairs, and to take off his great boots and to strip him.

"Is there a doctor near here, sir?" I asked.

"Right across the street; will I send my man?"

"Yes, and a-running, too," replied a comrade, who was stanching the blood on the man's chest with a bed-sheet.

We laid the man out, and I paused to note the splendor of the apartment, and to think it none too good for a brave soldier. The doctor came shortly, and I left the house. The troop was mounted and moved on. From a mansion across the street came a shot and loud shouting. We rode up and dismounted. There was a light in the front room and the door was open. The captain sprang up the steps, followed by ten or twelve men. As we entered we saw a half-dozen of the most vicious-looking wretches I have ever seen. They were evidently drunk, and did not comprehend the import of our presence. One man raised a champagne-bottle and threatened the captain. A carbine flashed—the report was almost deafening—and the drunken man dropped the bottle, threw up his hand, turned half round, and sank with a thud.

"Take these men out and shoot them, sergeant." And the now thoroughly terrorized revellers, to the number of six, were dragged, swearing and beseeching, to the pavement, and I heard shots.

The room we were in was magnificent, but in the utmost disorder. The floor was strewn with broken bottles, vases, and bric-à-brac.

A form appeared in the door. It was a woman. She was speechless with terror, and her eyes stared, and her hands were clutched. We removed our hats, and the woman closed her eyes slowly.

"Look out, captain, she's going to faint!" I cried.

The captain slapped his hat on with a crush.

"That's what she's going to do," he said, as he stood like a football-rusher before the ball is put in play.

"Grab her!" I shouted; and, with a bound, the captain made a high tackle just as the lady became limp. Out in the hall I jumped, and yelled, "Oh, you people up-stairs there, come down; come running; the lady has fainted; we are soldiers; come down; come down; come down, somebody!" And from the upper darkness a white-robed figure glided past me into the lighted room.

"Oh, I'm so glad!" she said, as she swept up to the rather engaging scene of the beautiful woman and the captain, who was "not glad," judging from his disconcerted air; and to make a story short, we left the house.

As we mounted we could see the darkness beginning to gray, and knew that morning would come shortly.

"It's been a nasty night's work, but if it once comes daylight I'll leave nothing of these rioters but their horrible memory," mused the old captain.

"There is a glow in the sky off there—don't you see?" I added.

"Fire! Oh, I've expected that."

As the light grayed I could see the doors of majestic residences open, windows broken, and débris trailing down the steps.

"Looted."

"There are people ahead—trot!" said the captain, half turning in his saddle. The bray of the trumpet was followed by the jingle of the forward movement.

The captain pulled off to the side and shouted, "No prisoners, men—no prisoners!" And the column swept along.

We could make out more human forms, all running by the side of the road. There were more and more fugitives as we drew nearer.

"Come on," sang out the first lieutenant, as he put his horse into a gallop and drew his six-shooter; and shortly we were among them, scattering them like chaff and firing revolver-shots into them. Up the side streets they went, scampering, terrorized.

"I guess they will keep that gait for a mile," said the lieutenant, as he turned grinning to me. "That is the outfit which has been looting down Michigan Avenue. I wish the light would come, and we'll give 'em hot stuff."

At Washington Park we dismounted, and shortly were joined by B Troop from Hordon's command. They told us they had been fighting all night, and that the stock-yards and many buildings were on fire. They had encountered opposition, which seemed to be armed and to have some organization, but, laughing, he said, "They couldn't stand the ' hot stuff.' "

After this we made the ride back. It was now light, and as we rode slowly, men dismounted at intervals, and did some pretty work at rather long ranges with the carbines. The enemy would see us coming, and start to run up side streets, and then, riding forward, we dismounted

and potted at them.   I saw a corporal " get a man " who
was running upwards of six blocks away—it was luck, of
course.   The police were now seen posted along at intervals, and were going into houses to tell the people of the
order to remain in-doors for twenty-four hours more,
which was the latest from headquarters, and I suppose
was intended to give the police and troops an opportunity
to seek out armed insurgents.

I got back to camp, dismounted, and, being hungry, bethought me of the Auditorium for breakfast.   I didn't
think, after the pounding the hotel had gotten in the
early evening previous, that they would come out strong
on an early breakfast, but they did fairly well.   You remember Ed Kennedy, the popular clerk there—well, he
was shot and badly wounded while behind the desk, after
the bomb drew our fire.   He will get around all right, I
am told.

I saw some of the execution of those hundreds of prisoners next day, but I didn't care to see much.   They
piled them on flat-cars as though they had been cord-
wood, and buried them out in the country somewhere.
Most of them were hobos, anarchists, and toughs of the
worst type, and I think they " left their country for their
country's good."   Chicago is thoroughly worked up now,
and if they keep with the present attention to detail,
they will have a fine population left.   The good citizens
have a monster vigilance committee, and I am afraid will
do many things which are not entirely just, but it is the
reaction from lawlessness, and cannot be helped.   They
have been terribly exasperated by the rioting and license
of the past.   Of course, my dear friend, all this never
really happened, but it all might very easily have happened if the mob had continued to monkey with the
military buzz-saw.   Yours faithfully,   JACK.

THE COLONEL OF THE FIRST CYCLE
INFANTRY

"YOU certainly are a tough outfit, colonel—you and your night-hawks of the First Bikes—and I am not sure you could not have us cavalrymen going to bed with our boots on, if we were on the other side," said Major Ladigo, as he bit at the end of a fresh cigar.

"Yes—bless me—Pedal's outfit might come into camp on top of yours, Ladigo, and where would my guns be then? I can't have my gunners sitting on their trails all day and all night too," sighed the big gunner, from the other end of the tent.

"It was good work," continued the old brigadier— "here, boy, pass those glasses—and I have always thought well of the possibilities of that machine in a certain sort of military operations. I don't think you can chase Apaches with it—in fact, the only way to chase Apaches is to agree to pay about $500 a head for them ; and, also, I don't think, Colonel Pedal—with all due respect for your enthusiasm—that you could ever become of all-absorbing interest in great operations between organized armies, but I do not want to commit myself since you seem to accomplish such feats in these days. If we had not had a really progressive man at the head of the army you would not have had this opportunity ; but now, Pedal, all these fellows want to hear about your outfit, and especially how you conducted that affair at North Colville — they all want to know—go ahead now—we have plenty of time to listen," and Colonel Pedal of the First Bikes twirled his forage cap in his two hands and grinned pleasantly.

" Well—it was simple enough," he said.

" Oh yes—it's simple now, but how did you get at it?" was the remark of encouragement from somewhere.

" Oh, well, you know, when I had organized and drilled this regiment, the people up at headquarters used me in a fussy way as orderlies, messengers, and in light outpost work, until my outfit was scattered all over this country, and that was not my idea at all. I knew by long experiment that bicycles were perfectly mobile in any country not strictly mountainous, and my idea was that I could fight my outfit in a new way; but fight it, that was my idea—and march it, too. I wanted a few holes in that flag, and so I used to go up and labor with the general. I pleaded and begged to be turned loose. So one afternoon the general sent for me, and I went to headquarters.

" He said that a big band of insurgents were gathering and organizing up at North Colville, and that he wanted them destroyed or dispersed, and asked me if I could do it without asking for supports. I knew the old man had all he could do to open the communications to the west, and that he was going to give the bikes a try to prove what they were good for, so I said 'Yes, sir,' right away, though I did not know the situation thoroughly; but I wanted a job of that sort, and I was in for it. So he gave me orders to that effect, and after some inquiries I left him. Through spies he knew of this condition, and that all the communications were cut except the marine cable, which he laid in the bed of the Kaween River to Northport, and that was thirty miles from North Colville. I knew that all those upper counties were in a state of insurgency, and my orders were to destroy the rendezvous

at North Colville and to then retreat; so my chief concern
was to get through the country without being stopped or
engaged seriously by intervening bodies of the enemy
which I might encounter, and says I to myself, says I,
'Old man, show 'em what bikes are good for.' Pardon
me if I become enthusiastic. I started down to my command, fell in my men, with two days' rations and one
hundred and fifty rounds. I made my inspection, for, of
course, you know, bike soldiers have a very complicated
equipment; what with bombs, telegraphic apparatus, tools,
and the extra parts of wheels, one must look well to his inspection. They have the Rice equipment—combined car-
tridge-belts and garment—which enables them to carry almost anything on the shoulder-belt. At five o'clock we
pulled out, and at dark found ourselves at our extreme outposts, as I had calculated. I did not want the enemy to see
me, as I was afraid of the telegraph, but as I proceeded I
tapped the wires and cut them again and again. In fact,
I cut wires all night, for fear that they might not have
been destroyed, or that they might have been repaired.
I ran smoothly through little hamlets, and knew that I
could not be overtaken. I made a slight detour around
villages of any size, such as Wooddale, Rockville, and
Freeport, for fear that the insurgents might be in force
enough to detain me. Back of Wellsville I got awfully
tangled up in a woods, and, in short, was lost; but I
jumped an old cit. out of his cosey bed, put a .45 on the
cabin of his intellect, a flash-lantern in his two eyes, and
he looked sufficiently honest and intelligent to show us
the road, which he did, and we were not detained long.

" I felt fear of Emmittstowne, as I had information that
the insurgents were in force there. We picked up a man
on the road who seemed to be one of our sympathizers,
and he informed us that there were pickets all along the

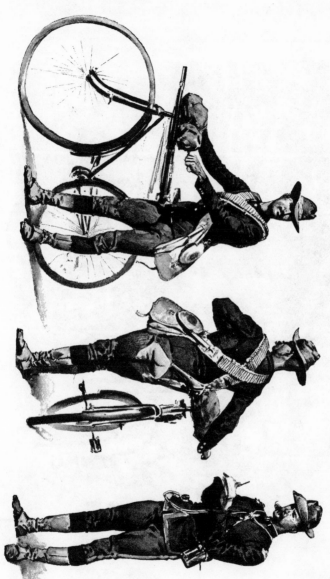

OFFICER AND MEN—FIRST CYCLE INFANTRY

AMBULANCE CORPS—FIRST CYCLE INFANTRY

road which we were travelling, and also mounted patrols. He said that there were a terrible lot of insurgents in Em-mittstowne, but mostly drunk.

"Captain Bidewell, who was in command of the advance, did a rather clever piece of work here. He suspected that he would find a picket at a certain place, and sent a dismounted squad on either side of the road, which was bounded by meadow land with stone-walls, brush, and trees on either side, and he himself walked down the road with two men. They talked loudly, as though drunk, and sure enough, were shortly held up by the picket. They surrendered and expostulated in a loud voice, and offered their captors a bottle of whiskey. The advance closed in on them and even got in their rear, and, of course, held up the picket without a shot. A six-shooter argument used on these people shortly disclosed the conditions, and we advanced."

"Say, colonel, I know that Bidewell; he is organizing a bike regiment out West now—met him as I came through," interpolated a medical major.

"Yes—nice fellow—held the ten-mile record for two years before this trouble," replied Pedal; "but, as I was saying—

"Here is *How!* gentlemen!

"Well, to continue — to show you a curious phase of bicycling—my advance ran a picket farther along the road and were fired on, but, bless me, they had gone through so quickly and silently that they were not hurt, and the ser-geant, who was very wise, dismounted and blew his whis-tle for us to advance. Bidewell dismounted and immedi-ately advanced, and the picket, hearing his men smashing brush, retreated, and the sergeant turned a pistol loose in their faces and bellowed for them to go out in the road, throw up their hands, and surrender, which they did. You

see, Colonel Ladigo, it is very hard to estimate bike
forces in the night, they go so silently—they simply flit;
and when you first notice them you wonder how many
have gone before. A sleepy picket is waked up by a lot
of bellowing and shots and smashing of brush, and he
doesn't know anything, especially if the row is half in his
rear. Well, the shooting must have aroused the village
of Emmittstowne, and I made up my mind to run right
into the town. The moon was rising, and we could see fairly
well; but first I tried a little ruse with the captured picket. We advanced down the road a piece, and the men ensconced themselves in the brush, while one of the captured
men stood in the middle of the road. We heard quite a
party coming up the road rapidly, and the picket called
out to them that it was nothing—that they had fired at
some shadows, and that they might go back. Two men
actually advanced to him, but he insisted that all was
right, and that they might return; in fact, he protested
too much, since he knew that he was lying for his life,
and that the date of his demise was fixed at the instant
he told the truth. We gave the town half an hour to
settle down, and then started on a down grade—coasting
silently. All was still. There were lights in a few sa-
loons, and a half-dozen men, who were immediately held
up and disarmed. There was evidence of a great many
people in the village, since wagons and horses stood about,
and tents and huts were everywhere except on the main
street. I stopped in front of the hotel, and, do you
know, my column got three-quarters of the way through
the town before we were discovered. My column is three-
quarters of a mile long, you must remember, and that
was very fortunate. Some one fired a shot from a dark-
ened window of the hotel, and I ordered my men to use
their revolvers. A man can shoot a revolver with great

accuracy from a wheel, as it glides so smoothly. Well, there was a deuce of a popping, and it must have fairly riddled the town. The fire was shortly returned, but in a desultory way which did not seem to do any damage, and shortly the tail of the column passed down the street. I had set the hotel on fire before we left, and I really do not think that those fellows know what really happened there yet. I immediately cut the telegraph line, and now had nothing to interfere with my march to North Colville. I had two bikes ruined by shots, and abandoned the riders; but they made their way to our lines later. As we proceeded the country grew more flat, and we made the pedals spin; at times we overtook night prowlers—tramps, for the most part—and one rather large party of drunken insurgents, all of whom we disarmed and left tied to trees and fences along the road. Do you know, Ladigo, that one cannot hear my whole regiment on a road until it is right on top of you. I have frequently seen men ride a bicycle right up beside a man, who never heard a word until ordered to throw up his hands."

"Oh yes, Pedal, I'd like to catch your outfit at the foot of a long hill; I would fire yellow-legs into you in a way you would despise," interpolated the impetuous cavalryman, as he blew smoke at the ridge-pole and slapped his one leg over the other in a satisfied way.

"Yes, you might, Ladigo; but I'm going to spend my life trying not to let you catch me at the foot of a long hill, and if you do, you will find about one hundred bicycles piled up in the road, and it makes bad travelling for horses, especially with unshaken infantry pointing at you from behind. Well, in this case, Ladigo, I did not have any of your enterprising yellow-legs to bother me. As I was saying, we went along swimmingly until we struck Cat-tail Creek, and found the bridge burned. It was rath-

er chilly, but I knew there was no help for it, so we got
out our air-cushions and did our little swimming drill right
there."

"What are your air-cushions?" inquired the medical
officer with the long pipe.

"They are made of rubber, and blow up, and will sustain
five equipments, and weigh fourteen pounds. Every five
men have one," explained Pedal.

"Oh, I see—a quaint scheme!"

"Yes; bikes are perfectly mobile," continued Pedal,
with satisfaction. "As I was saying—oh yes, we got over
the river all right, but—" and here he glanced appre-
hensively at Ladigo—"but I forgot to mention that we
lost fifteen bicycles in the passage."

"Ha—ha! oh yes—there are your dismounted men,"
and Colonel Ladigo beamed.

"I think horses would have stuck in the mud of Cat-
tail Creek, Ladigo; fact is, horses are not perfectly mobile.
I also neglected to mention that the bicycles were all
fished up and joined us later. We halted on a hill off the
road an hour before gray dawn, to wait for the command
to close up and to eat. There are always bikes which
break down, and it takes a little time to repair them; and
men will fall and injure themselves more or less. But
within an hour I had my command all up except five men,
having marched nearly seventy miles in eleven hours, had
one engagement, crossed a river. And now, Colonel Ladigo, was that not good work?"

"Oh yes, Pedal, quite good—quite good; could do it
myself, though," and the soul of a cavalryman was bound
to assert itself.

"Undoubtedly you could, but not next day." And Pedal
lit a cigar, conscious that he had Ladigo downed, but not
finally suppressed.

" My men down the road took in a cavalry patrol without a shot—actually took in a cavalry—"

" Hump—hump !" snorted Ladigo ; " cavalry forsooth—
a lot of d—— jays on plough-teams ; cavalry, sir—"

" Here—here, Ladigo, come down," expostulated the
assembled officers, and Ladigo relapsed.

" Well, after a reconnoissance and information from the
patrol, I found that there were over five thousand men
rendezvoused there, partly organized, and armed with all
sorts of guns. Old Middle was in command—you remember Middle, formerly of the Twenty - seventh Infantry,
cashiered at Fort Verde in '82."

He was known to the men present, and a few sniffs and
the remark that " he was bad medicine " was all that greeted the memory of Middle.

" From the patrol I found where their camps and lines
and outworks to cover the roads were, and also that it was
but a quarter of a mile across a wood-lot to the road which
I had intended to retire by, which ran southeast towards
Spearfish and Hallam Junction, so I trundled my bikes
over to it, and laid them in a column formation off the
road, and left them under guard.   I formed my command
and turned some fellows out of some rifle-pits, which were
designed to protect the road, and it was growing light.
We charged into the town, which had been alarmed by
our fire directed at the men in the pits.   The first thing
we struck was a long line of temporary camps, of what
was probably a regiment, which was on the other side of a
railroad embankment ; but they were in a panic and offered
us no resistance, while we advanced, rapidly firing, and
nearly destroyed them.   As we entered the town I took
one battalion and directed it against the car-shops, which
were full of stores and troops: these men we also nearly
destroyed ; and, having set fire to the shops, I entered the

main part of the town, and as we advanced I had it also fired. From my right I heard heavy firing, and knew that the other command had encountered opposition; and turning to my right I struck a second railroad embankment, swarming behind with men who were standing off the advance of the other battalion. I enfiladed them, and they retired precipitously. From the net-work of railroad embankments farther up the flats north of Colville I could see masses of men forming. They began firing at me from a great distance, but we were protected by the railroad fill and did not mind it; while our sharpshooters, with their arms of longer range, annoyed the enemy quite a little, and kept up his demoralization. A great many men had gotten away from the town when I had attacked the car-shops, and I was in fear lest they might form in my rear under the cover of the burning town, so I had my wounded removed rapidly to the hill where my bikes were left, and then retreated rapidly under the cover of the smoke. The enemy were left so completely in the air that they advanced slowly, while from the cover of the brush on the upper edge of a field I held them in play for an hour while my wounded got a good start. At last they seemed to form, and approached to my right, going around the smoke of the burning town, and as they outnumbered me four to one, they would speedily have outflanked me. I began the retreat as I had intended. I had thirty-eight badly wounded men who had to be carried in blankets, fifty-six slightly wounded who would be trundled on bicycles, and had left eighteen dead on the field."

"I say, colonel, how do you remove wounded men on bicycles?" asked some one.

"It is simple when you see it, but rather difficult to explain. If you will come down some day I will be glad to show you a wounded drill, and then you can see for your-

self.   By cutting sticks and tying a blanket or shelter-
tent a desperately wounded man can be laid prone between two bicycles, or if slightly hurt he can be trundled
or even ridden double with a comrade, while one man can
move two and even three bicycles.   Oh, I tell you, the
bike is a great contrivance once you come to understand it," proceeded the Colonel of Cycle Infantry.

"I should like to have fought those fellows a little harder, but I was sixty miles inside of their lines, and I knew
that to prolong the affair would mean that they would
be heavily reinforced, and besides this was my first expedition.   I had already destroyed the bigger half of the
enemy and burned the town,.and I did not apprehend a
vigorous pursuit.   What to do with my wounded was now
on my mind.   The country to the east of North Colville
is very broken, wild, and sparsely inhabited.   It had become necessary to abandon my wounded.   I selected a
point over twelve miles from our battle-ground, far back
from the unfrequented road, in a very wild spot in the
hills, and left every man not able to travel there, with all
our rations and two medical officers, with ten men as a
detail for the camp.   My trail of course continued, and
they were never suspected.   Coming to the valley of the
Spearfish I halted and slept my command until sundown,
and then started for our lines.   On the way I rode into
and demoralized a half-dozen bands of armed insurgents,
and struck our lines at five o'clock in the morning."

"What became of your wounded up there, colonel?"
asked the medical officer with the long pipe.

"The evening following Captain Barhandle with fifty
men started and made a successful march to their relief,
and left two more medical officers and a lot of medical stores
and rations, and came back three days after.   The camp
was never discovered, and was relieved when the general

here made his first expedition into Wood County. They had protected themselves from prowlers by waylaying the roads, and had a dozen prisoners in camp, together with a half-dozen milch cows. My bike men are excellent foragers, since they have been so much on outpost duty."

"Suppose, Colonel Pedal, you were forced to abandon your bicycles, what would you do?"

"We had a detachment on a scout the other day who were pressed into some bad country and had to abandon their machines, which they did by sinking them in Dead Creek, and the next day we went out and recovered them. If it is desired to utterly destroy them, it can be done in an instant by stepping on the wheel and 'buckling' it, or if you remove the chain, it is useless to any one but yourself," explained the colonel.

"Now, colonel, do you consider that you can move your men successfully in a hilly or mountainous country?" inquired Ladigo.

"In all candor, no—not to a good advantage. I can march uphill as fast as infantry, and go down at limited-express speed; but I really want a rather flat country with lots of roads. I am not particular as to the quality of the roads, so there are enough of them. I can move through snow which has been tracked down by teams; I can fly on the ice; and when it is muddy there is always an inch or so beside the road which is not muddy, and that is enough for me. A favorable place for a bicycle is along a railroad track—going in the centre or at one side. When suddenly attacked, my men can get out of the road like a covey of quail, and a bicycle can be trundled across the worst possible country as fast as a man can travel, for you see all the weight of the man's gun and pack are on the wheel, which runs without any appreciable resistance, and all bike men know how to throw a bicycle over a fence with ease, and my average march is eighty miles a day. Ladigo, remember—eighty miles a day. No kind of roads, no conditions of weather, or anything but superior force can stop my command for an instant, sir;" and the colonel of cavalry rose and added, "Colonel Pedal, will you have a drink with me?"

A MERRY CHRISTMAS IN A SIBLEY TEPEE

"Eat, drink, and be merry, for to-morrow we die."
Not a good excuse, but it has been sufficient on many occasions to be true. The soldier on campaign passes life
easily. He holds it in no strong grip, and the Merry
Christmas evening is as liable to be spent in the saddle in
fierce contact with the blizzard as in his cosey tepee with
his comrades and his scant cheer. The jug containing
the spirits of the occasion may have been gotten from a
town fifty miles away on the railroad. It is certainly not
the distillation of the summer sunlight, and is probably
"tough" enough stuff to mingle naturally with its surroundings; but if one "drinks no more than a sponge" he
may not have the jaded, retrospective feeling and the
moral mending on the day to come. To sit on a camp
chest, and to try and forget that the soldier's quart cup is
not filled with best in the market, and then to enter into
the full appreciation of the picturesque occasion, is to
forget that long marches, "bull meat," and sleepless,
freezing nights are in the background. Pleasant hours sit
so nicely in their complemental surrounding of hard ones,
since everything in the world is relative. As to the eating
in a cavalry camp on campaign, it is not overdone, for
beans and coffee and bacon and bacon and coffee and
beans come round with sufficient regularity to forestall
all gormandizing. The drinking is not the prominent

THE TOAST: "MERRY CHRISTMAS!"

feature either, but helps to soften the asperities of a Dakota blizzard which is raging on the other side of the
"ducking."

The Sibley tent weaves and moans and tugs frantically
at its pegs. The Sibley stove sighs like a furnace while the
cruel wind seeks out the holes and crevices. The soldiers
sit in their camp drawing-room buttoned up to the chin in
their big canvas overcoats, and the muskrat caps are not
removed. The freemasonry of the army makes strong
friendships, and soldiers are all good fellows, that being a
part of their business. There are just enough exceptions
to prove the rule. The cold, bloodless, compound-interest
snarler is not in the army, and if he were he would be as
cheerless on a damp evening as he would in a fight. One
man is from Arizona, another from Washington, and the
rest from the other corners of Uncle Sam's tract of land.
They have met before, and memory after memory comes
up with its laughter and pathos of the old campaigns.
One by one the "shoulder-straps" crawl in through the
hole in the tepee. And, mind you, they do not walk in
like a stage hero, with dash and abandon and head in the
air; they prostrate themselves like a Turk at prayer, and
come crawling. If they raise the flap ever so much, and
bring company of the Dakota winds, they are met with a
howl of protests. After gaining erectness, they brush the
snow from their clothes, borrow a tin cup, and say,
"How! how!"

The chief of scouts buttons up to his eyes, and must go
look after his "Inguns"; the officer of the day comes in
to make his papers, and if he keeps the flying jokes out
of his statistics, he does well enough. The second lieutenant, fresh from West Point, doesn't hesitate to address
the grizzled colonel of twenty campaigns—nay, he may
even deign to advise him on the art of war; but that is

unsatisfactory — the advising of colonels — because the colonel's advice to the sub has always to be acted upon, whereas the sub's advice to the colonel is mostly nullified by the great powers of discretion which are vested in the superior rank.   The life-study of a sub should be to appear like the cuckoo - bird in a German clock — at the proper moment; and when he appears at wrong intervals, he is repaired.   Colonels are terrible creatures, with vast powers for promoting happiness or inflicting misery.   If he will lend the moderating influence of his presence, it is well; but if he sends his man around to "present his compliments, and say that the d—— row will immediately cease," his wishes if not his personality are generally respected.

It is never a late evening, such a one as this; it's just a few stolen moments from the "demnition grind."   The last arrival may be a youngster just in from patrol, who explains that he just " cut the trail of forty or fifty Sioux five miles below, on the crossing of the White River;" and you may hear the bugle, and the bugle may blow quick and often, and if the bugle does mingle its notes with the howling of the blizzard, you will discover that the occasion is not one of merriment.   But let us hope that it will not blow.

The toasts go around, and you use your tobacco in a miserly way, because you can't get any more, since only to-day you have offered a dollar for a small plug to a trooper, and he had refused to negotiate, although he had pared off a small piece as a gift, and intimated that generosity could go no further.   Then you go to your tepee, half a mile down the creek at the scout camp, and you stumble through the snow-laden willows and face the cutting blast, while the clash and " Halt!" of the sentinel stop you here and there.   You pull off your boots and

crawl into your blankets quickly before the infernal Sibley·
stove gives its sigh as the last departing spark goes up the
chimney, and leaves the winds and drifting snows to bellow and scream over the wild wastes.

BEAR-CHASING IN THE ROCKY MOUNTAINS

MR. MONTAGUE STEVENS is an Englishman who for the most part attends to the rounding-up of his cattle, which are scattered over the northwestern quarter of New Mexico; but he does not let that interfere with the time which all Englishmen set duly apart to be devoted to sport. His door-yard is some hundreds of miles of mountain wilderness and desolate mesa—a more gorgeous preserve than any king ever dreamed of possessing for his pleasure—with its plains dotted with antelope, and its mountains filled with cougar, deer, bear, and wild turkeys. The white race has given up the contest with nature in those parts, and it has reverted to the bear, the Navajo, and Mr. Stevens—land-grants, corrals, cabins, brands, and all else.

General Miles was conducting a military observation of the country, which is bound to be the scene of any war which the Apaches or Navajos may make; and after a very long day's march, during which we had found but one water, and that was a pool of rain-water, stirred into mud and full of alkali, where we had to let our horses into the muddy stuff at the ends of our lariats, we had at last found a little rivulet and some green grass. The coffee-pot bubbled and the frying-pan hissed, while I smoked and listened to a big escort-wagon driver, who was repairing his lash, and saying, softly, "Been drivin' a bloody lot of burros for thirty years, and don't know enough to keep a whip out of a wheel; guess I'll go to jack-punchin', 'nen I kin use a dry club."

Far down the valley a little cloud of dust gleamed up against the gray of the mountains, and presently the tireless stride of a pony shone darkly in its luminous midst. Nearer and nearer it grew—the flying tail, the regular beating of the hoofs, the swaying figure of the rider, and the left sleeve of the horseman's coat flapping purposelessly about. He crossed the brook with a splash, trotted, and, with a jerk, pulled up in our midst. Mr. Stevens is a tall, thin young man, very much bronzed, and with the set, serious face of an Englishman. He wore corduroy clothes, and let himself out of his saddle with one hand, which he also presented in greeting, the other having been sacrificed to his own shot-gun on some previous occasion. Mr. Stevens brought with him an enthusiasm for bear which speedily enveloped the senses of our party, and even crowded out from the mind of General Miles the nobler game which he had affected for thirty years.

The steady cultivation of one subject for some days is bound to develop a great deal of information, and it is with difficulty that I refrain from herein setting down facts which can doubtless be found in any good encyclopædia of natural history; but the men in the mountains never depart from the consideration of that and one other subject, which is brands, and have reached some strange conclusions — the strangest being that the true Rocky Mountain grizzly is only seen once in a man's lifetime, and that the biggest one they ever heard of leaves his tracks in this district, and costs Mr. Stevens, roughly estimating, about $416 a year to support, since that about covers the cattle he kills.

At break of day the officers, cavalrymen, escort-wag-

WATERING HORSES

ons, and pack-train toiled up the Cañon Largo to Mr. Stevens's camp, which was reached in good time, and consisted of a regular ranchman's grub-wagon, a great many more dogs of more varieties than I could possibly count, a big Texan, who was cook, and a professional bear-hunter by the name of Cooper, who had recently departed from his wonted game for a larger kind, with the result that, after the final deal, a companion had passed a .45 through Mr. Cooper's face and filled it with powder, and brought him nigh unto death, so that even now Mr. Cooper's head was swathed in bandages, and his mind piled with regrets that he had on at the time an overcoat, which prevented him from drawing his gun with his usual precision. Our introduction to the outfit was ushered in by a most magnificent free-for-all dog-fight; and when we had carefully torn the snarling, yelling, biting mass apart by the hind-legs and staked them out to surrounding trees, we had time to watch Mr. Cooper draw diagrams of bear-paws in the dust with a stick. These tracks he had just discovered up the Cañon Largo, and he averred that the bear was a grizzly, and weighed 1800 pounds, and that he had been there two years, and that all the boys had hunted him, but that he was a sad old rascal.

After lunch we pulled on up the cañon and camped. The tents were pitched and the cooks busy, when I noticed three cowboys down the stream and across the cañon, who were alternately leading their horses and stooping down in earnest consultation over some tracks on the ground. We walked over to them. There were Mr. Cooper, whose only visible eye rolled ominously, and Dan, the S. U. foreman, with another puncher.

"He's usin' here," said Cooper. "That's his track, and there's his work," pointing up the hill-side, where lay the body of a five-year-old cow. We drew near her, and

there was the tale of a mighty struggle, all written out
more eloquently than pen can do.   There were the deep
furrows of the first grapple at the top; there was the
broad trail down the steep hill for fifty yards, with the
stones turned over, and the dust marked with horn and
hoof and claw; and there was the stump which had broken the roll down hill.   The cow had her neck broken
and turned under her body; her shoulder was torn from
the body, her leg broken, and her side eaten into; and
there were Bruin's big telltale footprints, rivalling in size
a Gladstone bag, as he had made his way down to the
stream to quench his thirst and continue up the cañon.
The cow was yet warm—not two hours dead.

"DO YOU THINK THIS PONY IS GOING TO BUCK?"

"We must pull out of here; he will come back to-night," said Cooper. And we all turned to with a will and struck the tents, while the cooks threw their tins, bags, and boxes into the wagons, whereat we moved off down wind for three miles, up a spur of the cañon, where we again camped. We stood around the fires and allowed Mr. Cooper to fill our minds with hope. "He'll shore come back; he's usin' here; an' cow outfits—why, he don't consider a cow outfit nothin'. He's been right on top of cow outfits since he's been in these parts, and thet two years gone now, when he begun to work this yer range, and do the work you see done yonder. In the mornin' we'll strike his trail, and if we can git to him you'll shore see a bar-fight."

We turned in, and during the night I was awakened twice—once by a most terrific baying of all the dogs, who would not be quieted, and later by a fine rain beating in my face. The night was dark, and we were very much afraid the rain would kill the scent. We were up long before daylight, and drank our coffee and ate our meat, and as soon as "we could see a dog a hundred yards," which is the bear-hunter's receipt, we moved off down the creek. We found that the cow had been turned over twice, but not eaten—evidently Bruin had his suspicions. The dogs cut his trail again and again. He had run within sight of our camp, had wandered across the valley hither and yon, but the faithful old hounds would not "go away." Dan sat on his pony and blew his old cow's horn, and yelled: "Hooick! hooick! get down on him, Rocks; hooick! hooick!" But Rocks could not get down on him, and then we knew that the rain had killed the scent. We circled a half-mile out, but the dogs were still; and then we followed up the Cañon Largo for miles, and into the big mountain, through juniper thickets and

DAN AND ROCKS

over malpais, up and down the most terrible places, for
we knew that the bear's bed-ground is always up in the
most rugged peaks, where the rimrock overhangs in ser-
ried battlements, tier on tier. But no bear.

Rocks, the forward hound, grew weary of hunting for
things which were not, and retired to the rear to pay
court to a lady friend; and Dan had to rope Rocks, and
with some irritation he started his pony, and Rocks
kept the pace by dint of legging it, and by the help of a
tow from 900 pounds of horse-flesh. Poor Rocks! He
understood his business; but in consequence of not being able to explain to the men what fools they were, he
suffered.

The hot mid-day sun of New Mexico soon kills the
scent, and we were forced to give over for the day. A
cavalry sergeant shot three deer, but we, in our superior purpose, had learned to despise deer. Later I
made a good two-hundred-yard centre on an antelope,
and though I had not been fortunate enough in years to

get an antelope, the whole sensation was flat in view of this new ambition.

On the following morning we went again to our dead cow, but nothing except the jackals had been at the bear's prey, for the wily old fellow had evidently scented our camp, and concluded that we were not a cow outfit, whereat he had discreetly "pulled his freight."

We sat on our horses in a circle, and raised our voices. In consideration of the short time at our disposal, we concluded that we could be satisfied with taking 1800 pounds of bear on the instalment plan. The first instalment was a very big piece of meat, but was—I am going to confess —presented to us in the nature of a gift; but the whole thing was so curious I will go into it.

We hunted for two days without success, unless I include deer and antelope; but during the time I saw two things which interested me. The first was a revelation of the perfect understanding which a mountain cow-pony has of the manner in which to negotiate the difficulties of the country which is his home.

Dan, the foreman, was the huntsman. He was a shrewd-eyed, little, square-built man, always very much preoccupied with the matter in hand. He wore a sombrero modelled into much character by weather and time, a corduroy coat, and those enormous New-Mexican "chaps," and he sounded a cow-horn for his dogs, and alternately yelped in a most amusing way. So odd was this yelp that it caught the soldiers, and around their camp-fire at night you could hear the mimicking shouts of "Oh, Rocks! eh-h-h! hooick! get down on him, Rocks; tohoot! tohoot!" We were sitting about on our horses in a little *sienneca*, while Dan was walking about, leading his pony and looking after his dogs.

When very near me he found it necessary to cross an

A DANGEROUS PLACE

"GONE AWAY"

arróyo which was about five feet deep and with perfectly perpendicular banks. Without hesitation he jumped down into it, and with a light bound his pony followed. At the opposite side Dan put up his arms on the bank and clawed his way up, and, still paying no attention to his pony, he continued on. Without faltering in the least, the little horse put his fore-feet on the bank, clawed at it once, twice, jumped, scratched, clawed, and, for all the world like a cat getting into the fork of a tree, he was on the bank and following Dan.

Later in the day, when going to our camp, we followed one of Dan's short-cuts through the mountains, and the cowboys on their mountain ponies rode over a place which made the breath come short to the officers and men behind; not that they could not cross themselves, being on foot, but that the cavalry horses could they had their solemn doubts, and no one but an evil brute desires to lead a game animal where he may lose his life. Not being a geologist, I will have to say it was a blue clay in process of rock formation, and in wet times held a mountain torrent. The slope was quite seventy degrees. The approach was loose dirt and malpais, which ran off down the gulch in small avalanches under our feet. While crossing, the horses literally stood on their toes to claw out a footing. A slip would have sent them, belly up, down the toboggan-slide, with a drop into an unknown depth at the end. I had often heard the cavalry axiom "that a horse can go anywhere a man can if the man will not use his hands," and a little recruit murmured it to reassure himself. I passed, with the loss of a quarter of the skin on my left hand, and later asked a quaint old veteran of four enlistments if he thought it was a bad place, and he said, " It's lizards, not harses, what ought to go thar."

Riding over the rough mountains all day sows poppyseeds in a man's head, and when the big medical officer opens your tent-flaps in the morning, and fills the walls with his roars to "Get up! it's four o'clock," it is with groans that you obey. You also forego washing, because you are nearly frozen stiff, and you go out and stand around the fire with your companions, who are all cheerfully miserable as they shiver and chaff each other. It seems we do not live this life on a cold, calculating plane of existence, but on different lines, the variation of which is the chief delight of the discriminating, and I must record a distinct pleasure in elbowing fellows around a camp-fire when it is dark and cold and wet, and when you know that they are oftener in bed than out of it at such hours. You drink your quart of coffee, eat your slice of venison, and then regard your horse with some trepidation, since he is all of a tremble, has a hump on his back, and is evidently of a mind to "pitch."

The eastern sky grows pale, and the irrepressible Dan begins to "honk" on his horn, and the cavalcade moves off through the grease-wood, which sticks up thickly from the ground like millions of Omaha war-bonnets.

The advance consists of six or eight big blood-hounds, which range out in front, with Dan and Mr. Cooper to blow the horn, look out for "bear sign," and to swear gently but firmly when the younger dogs take recent deer trails under consideration. Three hundred yards behind come Scotch stag-hounds, a big yellow mastiff, fox-terriers, and one or two dogs which would not classify in a bench-show, and over these Mr. Stevens holds a guiding hand, while in a disordered band come General Miles, his son, three army officers, myself, and seven orderlies of the Second Cavalry. All this made a picture, but, like all Western canvases, too big for a frame. The sun broke in a golden flash over the hills, and streaked the

plain with gold and gray greens. The spirit of the thing
is not hunting but the chase of the bear, taking one's
mind back to the buffalo, or the nobles of the Middle
Ages, who made their "image of war" with bigger game
than red foxes.

Leaving the plain we wound up a dry creek, and noted
that the small oaks had been bitten and clawed down by
bear to get at the acorns. The hounds gave tongue, but
could not get away until we had come to a small glade in
the forest, where they grew wildly excited. Mr. Cooper
here showed us a very large bear track, and also a smaller
one, with those of two cubs by its side. With a wild burst
the dogs went away up a cañon, the blood went into our
heads, and our heels into the horses, and a desperate
scramble began. It is the sensation we have travelled so
long to feel. Dan and Cooper sailed off through the
brush and over the stones like two old crows, with their
coat-tails flapping like wings. We follow at a gallop in
single file up the narrow, dry watercourse. The creek
ends, and we take to the steep hill-sides, while the loose
stones rattle from under the flying hoofs. The rains
have cut deep furrows on their way to the bed of the
cañon, and your horse scratches and scrambles for a foothold. A low, gnarled branch bangs you across the face,
and then your breath fairly stops as you see a horse go
into the air and disappear over a big log, fallen down a
hill of seventy degrees' slope. The "take-off and land-
ing" is yielding dust, but the blood in your head puts the
spur in your horse, and over you go. If you miss, it is a
200-foot roll, with a 1200-pound horse on top of you.
But the pace soon tells, and you see nothing but good
honest climbing ahead of you. The trail of the yelling
dogs goes straight up, amid scraggly cedar and juniper,
with loose malpais underfoot. We arrive at the top only

TIMBER-TOPPING IN THE ROCKIES

to see Cooper and Dan disappear over a precipice after the dogs, but here we stop. Bears always seek the very highest peaks, and it is better to be there before them if possible. A grizzly can run downhill quicker than a horse, and all hunters try to get above them, since if they are big and fat they climb slowly; besides, the mountain-tops are more or less flat and devoid of underbrush, which makes good running for a horse. We scatter out along the cordon of the range. The bag doing on the rimrock of the mountain-tops, where the bear tries to throw off the dogs, makes it quite impossible to follow them at speed, so that you must separate and take your chances of heading the chase.

I selected Captain Mickler—the immaculate, the polo-player, the epitome of staff form, the trappiest trooper in the Dandy Fifth—and, together with two orderlies, we started. Mickler was mounted on a cow-pony, which measured one chain three links from muzzle to coupling. Mickler had on English riding-togs—this is not saying that the pony could not run, or that Mickler was not humorous. But it was no new experience for him, this pulling a pony and coaxing him to attempt breakneck experiments, for he told me casually that he had led bare-footed cavalrymen over these hills in pursuit of Apaches at a date in history when I was carefully conjugating Latin verbs.

We were making our way down a bad formation when we heard the dogs, and presently three shots. A strayed cavalry orderly had, much to his disturbance of mind, beheld a big silver-tip bearing down on him, jaws skinned, ears back, and red-eyed, and he had promptly removed himself to a proper distance, where he dismounted. The bear and dogs were much exhausted, but the dogs swarmed around the bear, thus preventing a shot. But Bruin stopped at intervals to fight the dogs, and the soldier fired, but without effect. If men do not come up with the dogs in order to encourage them, many will draw off, since the work of chasing and fighting a bear without water for hours is very trying. Only hounds can be depended on, as the tongues of other dogs thicken, and they soon droop when long without water. Some

of the dogs may have followed the bear with cubs, but
if they did we never heard of them. The one now running was an enormous silver-tip, and could not "tree."
The shots of the trooper diverted the bear, which now
took off down a deep cañon next to the one we were in,
and presently we heard him no more. After an hour's
weary travelling down the winding way we came out on
the plain, and found a small cow outfit belonging to Mr.
Stevens, and under a tree lay our dead silver-tip, while a
half-dozen punchers squatted about it. It appeared that
three of them had been working up in the foot-hills when
they heard the dogs, and shortly discovered the bear.
Having no guns, and being on fairly good ground, they
coiled their *riatas* and prepared to do battle.

The silver-tip was badly blown, and the three dogs
which had stayed with him were so tired that they sat up
at a respectful distance and panted and lolled. The first
rope went over Bruin's head and one paw. There lies the
danger. But instantly number two flew straight to the
mark, and the ponies surged, while Bruin stretched out
with a roar. A third rope got his other hind-leg, and the
puncher dismounted and tied it to a tree. The roaring,
biting, clawing mass of hair was practically helpless, but
to kill him was an undertaking.

"Why didn't you brand him and turn him loose?" I
asked of the cowboy.

"Well," said the puncher, in his Texan drawl, "we
could have branded him all right, but we might have
needed some help in turning him loose."

They pelted him with malpais, and finally stuck a
knife into a vital part, and then, loading him on a pony,
they brought him in. It was a daring performance, but
was regarded by the "punchers" as a great joke.

Mickler and I rode into camp, thinking on the savagery

of man.   One never heard of a bear which travelled all
the way from New Mexico to Chicago to kill a man, and
yet a man will go 3000 miles to kill a bear—not for love
or fear or hate or meat; for what, then?   But Mickler
and I had not killed a bear, so we were easy.

One by one the tired hunters and dogs struggled into
camp all disappointed, except the dogs, which could not
tell us what had befallen them since morning.   The day
following the dogs started a big black bear, which made a
good run up a bad place in the hills, but with the hunters
scrambling after in full cry.   The bear treed for the dogs,
but on sighting the horsemen he threw himself backward
from the trunk and fell fifteen feet among the dogs,
which latter piled into him *en masse*, the little fox-terriers being particularly aggressive.   It was a tremendous
shake-up of black hair and pups of all colors; but the
pace was too fast for Bruin, and he sought a new tree.
One little foxie had been rolled over, and had quite a job
getting his bellows mended.   This time the bear sat on a
limb very high up, and General Miles put a .50-calibre ball
through his brain, which brought him down with a tremendous thump, when the pups again flew into him, and
" wooled him," as the cowboys put it, to their hearts'
content.

While our bear-hunting is not the thing we are most
proud of, yet the method is the most sportsmanlike, since
nothing but the most desperate riding will bring one up
with the bear in the awful country which they affect.
The anticipation of having a big silver-tip assume the aggressive at any moment is inspiriting.   Indeed, they often
do ; for only shortly before one had sprung from a thicket
on to the hind-quarters of one of Mr. Stevens's cowboy's
ponies, and it was only by the most desperate work on the
part of his companion, who rode up close and shot the

bear with his six-shooter, that saved his comrade's life.
The horse was killed.   When one thinks of the enormous
strength of the silver-tip, which can overpower the mighti-
est steer, and bend and break its neck or tear its shoulder

THE FINALE

from its body at a stroke, one is able to say, "Do not
hunt a bear unless thy skin is not dear to thee."   Then
the dogs must be especially trained to run bear, since the
country abounds in deer, and it is difficult to train dogs
to ignore their sight and scent.   The cowboys account

THE RETURN OF THE HUNTERS

for the number of the bear in their country from the fact that it is the old Apache and Navajo range, and the incoherent mind of the savage was impressed with the rugged mass of fur and the grinning jaws of the monster which crossed his path, and he was awed by the dangers of the encounter—arrow against claw. He came to respect the apparition, and he did not know that life is only sacred when in the image of the Creator. He did not discriminate as to the value of life, but with his respect for death there grew the speculation, which to him became a truth, that the fearsome beast was of the other world, and bore the lost souls of the tribe. He was a vampire; he was sacred. O Bear!

THE END